# The Weekend Cook

# The Weekend Cook

SPEND YOUR WEEKEND ON
A GASTRONOMIC ADVENTURE

This edition published by Parragon Books Ltd in 2015
LOVE FOOD is an imprint of Parragon Books Ltd

Parragon Books Ltd
Chartist House
15–17 Trim Street
Bath BA1 1HA, UK
www.parragon.com/lovefood

ISBN 978-1-4723-9252-7

Printed in China

Introduction and extra text written by Anne Sheasby
Cover photography by Haarala Hamilton

*Notes for the Reader*
This book uses both metric and imperial measurements. Follow the same units of measurement
throughout; do not mix metric and imperial. All spoon measurements are level: teaspoons are assumed
to be 5 ml, and tablespoons are assumed to be 15 ml. Unless otherwise stated, milk is assumed to
be full fat, eggs and individual vegetables are medium, pepper is freshly ground black pepper and
salt is table salt. Unless otherwise stated, all root vegetables should be peeled prior to using.

The times given are an approximate guide only. Preparation times differ according to the
techniques used by different people and the cooking times may also vary from those given.

# Contents

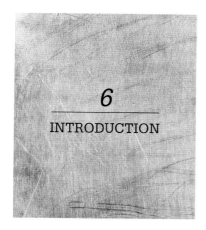

## 6
INTRODUCTION

## 12
FRIDAY NIGHT
GLOBAL TAKEAWAY

## 48
SATURDAY KICKSTART
BREAKFASTS & LUNCHES

## 78
SATURDAY EVENING
SPECIALS

## 138
SUNDAY BEST
EVER BRUNCH

## 166
SUNDAY LONG
& LAZY LUNCHES

## 192
WEEKEND BRILLIANT
BREADS

## 208
MONDAY MORNING
BOOSTERS

## 220
INDEX

# Introduction

*Weekends are important, so make yours count by turning mealtimes into edible adventures. Shake off the week and kick back with a selection of mind-blowing recipes that will transform your cooking repertoire from mundane to magic. Make the most of everyday ingredients and look forward to eating meals you'll never forget.*

This inspiring book is perfect for cooks who look forward to spending the weekend getting creative in the kitchen and experimenting with exciting new flavours. Whether you are planning a Friday night in with your version of a takeaway, or are inviting people over for a decadent dinner party, it's the only cookbook you'll need when the weekend arrives!

We'll take you on a culinary journey through the weekend, tempting you along the way with a fantastic choice of dishes, some relatively straightforward and others more challenging. There is something to suit all the more adventurous cooks out there and those who enjoy venturing further afield to hunt out unusual ingredients and create impressive dishes that demand a bit more time. This book is for visionary cooks who enjoy experimenting and want to create lasting food memories.

Friday night is the beginning of the weekend wind-down, so we start with a sizzling selection of tempting takeaway-style dishes from all over the world that are sure to get the weekend off to a great start. Rather than reaching for the usual takeaway menu, why not spend a bit of time rustling up one of these awesome options that will put your Friday-night menu on the food map?

Then, to kick things off on a Saturday, we include a savvy selection of breakfasts and lunches to set you up perfectly for whatever the day has in store. This section features a variety of options, from power-packed recipes to sustain your weekend energy to nutty mini muffins and a choice of brilliant bagels, butties and wraps. For those fitness fans who enjoy a Saturday morning workout, we also include a couple of power drinks to give you a boost before you start.

A chapter on Saturday evening specials covers all things extravagant, and encourages the adventurous cook in you to go the extra mile and create some amazing meals to share. This incredible selection of impressive, lavish main courses and to-die for desserts is sure to result in an onslaught of compliments from your hugely impressed guests. Plus, you'll relish the opportunity to push the boat out and experiment with new ideas every weekend.

Next up we feature some brilliant brunch dishes that are perfect for a relaxed Sunday morning, such as eggs, pancakes, frittatas, tarts, platters and even a few cheeky cocktails. With these recipes, you can show off your flair for creating the best-ever brunches that will have your friends queuing up outside your door, keen to sample your culinary skills and enjoy the chance to chill out over some delicious dishes.

Get set to impress on a Sunday with one of our long and lazy lunches, ideal for taking your time over. We feature a selection of savoury and sweet options, including classic roasts as well as slow-cooked meals, plus tempting desserts to satisfy any sweet cravings.

For all budding bakers out there, the next chapter on breads for the weekend is ideal for you. It's hard to resist the unmistakable aroma of freshly baked bread, so now you can try your hand at creating some bistro-style breads to serve up to your guests.

We even include a final chapter encompassing a few recipes to boost your mood, and your energy levels, and ensure your Monday morning kicks off with a blast, including rejuvenating juices, energy biscuits and power snacks.

So, if you're a food fanatic who relishes spending time experimenting with recipes and ingredients, creating food you love to eat, then you'll enjoy this culinary journey through a sensational selection of mind-blowing dishes.

# Top Tips for Weekend Cooking

*On Saturday morning, take some time out to visit your local farmers' market to see what culinary treats and interesting foods are on offer. Farmers' markets are typically home to a wide variety of high quality producers of delicious food and drink, giving you the opportunity to buy local produce direct from the supplier. You can wander around savouring the aromas and flavours from the samples on offer, and try out some mouth-watering new ingredients in readiness for creating some tasty meals for the weekend.*

It's also worth checking out nearby farm shops and local specialist or artisan food suppliers. It's amazing to discover the wide range of foods on your doorstep, so do make good use of these food fanatics in your region. In season, pick-your-own farms offer welcome gluts of fresh fruit and vegetables, providing plenty of produce and lots of inspiration for weekend cooking.

All year round, local fruit and vegetable markets offer seasonal produce as well as some more unusual things to try. Local butchers and fishmongers are well worth a visit if you are looking for something specific or simply wanting to get some inspiration. They can offer valuable advice on suitable cooking techniques and recipes for the various cuts of meat or fish, be it a simple idea or a more adventurous one. Artisan bakers, too, are good for baking inspiration and ideas, or if you just fancy a great-tasting loaf of bread or rolls to accompany lunch. They often stock fresh yeast too. Many supermarkets also have trained experts on hand to offer tips of their trade.

Specialist food markets, fairs and festivals are great places to visit and discover new food trends and ingredients. The variety of products on offer, as well as all the enticing aromas wafting around, will provide a truly awesome assault on your senses.

If you are lucky enough to live near Asian, Greek, Italian, Mexican, Polish or other specialist supermarkets, food stores or delis, take a look at the amazing array of fresh, dried, frozen and storecupboard items they have to offer – the wide choice will provide you with endless opportunities to get experimenting in the kitchen. Taste samples on offer and choose something that you perhaps haven't thought of trying before.

Try to be organized and have some idea of what meals you are planning before you venture out to do the shopping. But do allow some flexibility when selecting ingredients too, in case a new or interesting ingredient sparks off a slightly different idea or direction to go in.

Be bold and courageous and try your hand at new cooking techniques. Every couple of weekends or so, why not set yourself a target or challenge to try a new skill and add to your ever-increasing repertoire of recipes? Aim to challenge yourself without overstretching your skills.

The weekend is also the ideal time for experimenting with new kitchen gadgets, appliances and bits of kit that you have recently bought. Take the time to get familiar with the appliance and see what culinary wonders you can create with its help.

It's a good idea to plan and manage your time in the kitchen, so you have plenty of scope for preparing and cooking your meal, as well as enough time for experimenting and enjoying the whole process as well. Allow some time for trying out something new, plus ample time to relax and kick back along the way as well. Prepare things in advance where possible so you have more time to spend with friends, or get your guests involved with the cooking, so you can enjoy their company over a few beers as you cook together.

Above all, use this brilliant book to showcase your skills, flaunt your flair and impress your guests with your competent and creative cooking!

# Friday Night
## Global Takeaway

*It's Friday night and after a frantic week at work, it's time to wind down, chill out and enjoy a casual Friday night dinner. Once you head home from work, you will want to make the most of a relaxed evening in, so a home-made version of a classic takeaway will hit the spot and satisfy any hunger pangs. Most of these recipes can be knocked up fairly easily and any fresh ingredients that you'll need can be picked up at the supermarket or local deli or store on your way home from work.*

*Friday night is the perfect time to chill out with a group of friends or spend a quiet evening in, so whatever the occasion or company, we include a tempting collection of popular takeaway dishes from around the globe, from burgers and pizzas to kebabs and curries.*

You can also create some simple accompaniments to serve alongside these recipes, which can be knocked up easily and without too much effort. These could be fresh crusty bread, steamed rice, baked potato wedges or naan bread, winter or summer slaw, a mixed leaf or seasonal salad tossed in a zingy dressing, as well as one or two of your finest home-made chutneys, pickles, salsas or flavoured mustard or mayo. Or for something a bit different, check out one of the sauce recipes on offer, like Chipotle Ketchup or Chipotle Mustard.

We've got it all covered, so why not start by inviting your friends round and impressing them with a firm favourite like Cheeseburgers with Chips or the ever-popular Beer-battered Fish & Chips? Side orders of ketchup and mustard are all you'll need to complete the meal.

If an impromptu or casual dinner party is more your thing for a Friday night, try tempting guests to the table with flavourful dishes from afar, including Chicken Chow Mein from China, Pork Pad Thai from Thailand or Chipotle Pork Fajitas from Mexico.

For big appetites and those who favour a bit of extra heat and spice in their food, recipes such as Colossal Lamb Kebab with Hot Chilli Sauce or Blazing Hot Wings with Blue Cheese Dressing are guaranteed to hit the spicy spot.

On the other hand, if you decide to opt for a fun Friday movie night, sophisticated snacks including Rosemary, Sea Salt & Sesame Popcorn or Root Vegetable Crisps are sure to tantalize the taste buds.

So, whatever the occasion, or the company you are in, this chapter features something delicious for everyone to enjoy. Check out our feature on savvy storecupboard spices too, where we offer on-trend tips for how to add maximum flavour to dishes to create tasty meals after work.

So, as the working week draws to a close and Friday night marks the beginning of a great weekend ahead, all you have to do is to decide on your food mood, select the recipe of your choice, pour yourself a glass of something chilled, put your favourite background music on and let the creative cooking begin…

# Cheeseburgers with Chips

The secret to making top-notch chips is to double-fry them, so it's well worth the extra bit of effort to make these delicious home-made fries to serve alongside the succulent griddled cheeseburgers.

**SERVES 4**
Prepares in 30–35 minutes,
  plus soaking and cooling
Cooks in 55 minutes–1 hour
  10 minutes

## Cheeseburgers
750 g/1 lb 10 oz fresh beef mince
1 beef stock cube
1 tbsp minced dried onion
2 tbsp water
1–2 tbsp sunflower oil
55 g/2 oz Cheddar cheese, grated
lettuce leaves
4 burger buns, split
tomato slices

## Chips
675 g/1 lb 8 oz large potatoes
sunflower, corn or groundnut oil,
  for deep-frying
salt and pepper

1. To make the cheeseburgers, place the beef mince into a large mixing bowl. Crumble the stock cube over the beef mince, add the dried onion and water and mix well with a metal spoon to combine.

2. Divide the meat into four portions, shape each into a ball, then flatten slightly to make a patty of your preferred thickness.

3. Place a griddle pan over a medium–high heat. Lightly brush the burgers with oil and cook for 5–6 minutes. Turn the burgers, sprinkle the cheese over the cooked side and cook for a further 5–6 minutes, or until cooked to your liking. Set aside and keep warm.

4. To make the chips, peel the potatoes and cut into 8-mm/⅜-inch even-sized fingers. As soon as they are prepared, put them into a large bowl of cold water to prevent discoloration, then leave them to soak for 30 minutes to remove the excess starch.

5. Drain the potatoes and dry thoroughly on a clean tea towel. Preheat the oil in a deep-fat fryer or large, heavy-based saucepan to 190°C/375°F. If you do not have a thermometer, test the temperature by dropping a potato finger into the oil. If it sinks, the oil isn't hot enough; if it floats and the oil bubbles around the potato, it is ready.

6. Carefully add a small batch of potatoes to the oil (this is to ensure even cooking and to avoid reducing the temperature of the oil) and deep-fry for 5–6 minutes, or until softened but not browned. Remove from the oil and drain well on kitchen paper.

7. Leave the chips to cool for at least 5 minutes. Continue to deep-fry the remaining potatoes in the same way, allowing the oil to return to the correct temperature each time.

8. When ready to serve the chips, reheat the oil to 200°C/400°F. Add the potatoes in small batches and deep-fry for 2–3 minutes until golden brown. Remove from the oil and drain on kitchen paper.

9. To serve, place the lettuce leaves on the bottom halves of the burger buns and top with the cheeseburgers. Place a couple of tomato slices on top of the burger and add the bun lids. Season the chips to taste with salt and pepper, then serve alongside the burgers.

# Beer-battered Fish & Chips

*The bubbles in the beer add body and lightness to this super-crispy batter that encases the moist and succulent fish fillets inside. Served with hand-cut chips and mushy peas, this firm favourite is great for sharing with friends.*

**SERVES 4**
Prepares in 30 minutes,
 plus chilling and soaking
Cooks in 35–40 minutes

vegetable oil, for deep-frying
6 large potatoes, cut into thick chips and
 soaked (as described on page 17)
4 thick cod fillets, about 175 g/6 oz each
salt and pepper
lemon wedges, to serve

### Batter
225 g/8 oz self-raising flour,
 plus extra for dusting
½ tsp salt
300 ml/10 fl oz cold lager

### Mushy Peas
350 g/12 oz frozen peas
30 g/1 oz butter
2 tbsp single cream
salt and pepper

1. To make the batter, sift the flour into a bowl with the salt and whisk in most of the lager. Add the remaining lager; it should be thick, like double cream. Chill in the refrigerator for half an hour.

2. To make the mushy peas, cook the peas in lightly salted boiling water for 3 minutes. Drain and mash to a thick purée, add the butter and cream and season to taste. Set aside and keep warm.

3. Heat the oil to 120°C/250°F in a deep-fat fryer or a large, heavy-based saucepan. Preheat the oven to 150°C/300°F/Gas Mark 2. Fry the chips for about 8–10 minutes, or until softened but not coloured. Drain on kitchen paper and place in a dish in the oven. Increase the temperature of the oil to 180°C/350°F.

4. Season the fish to taste and dust lightly with flour. Dip one fillet in the batter and coat thickly. Carefully place in the hot oil and repeat with the other fillets. Cook for 8–10 minutes, turning over halfway through. Drain and keep warm.

5. Reheat the oil to 180°C/350°F and recook the chips for 2–3 minutes, or until golden brown and cooked through. Drain and season to taste. Serve the chips with the fish, mushy peas and lemon wedges for squeezing over.

# Margherita Pizza

*Make the dough for this tasty pizza as soon as you get home from work and leave it to rise as you wind down. Then get cracking on the topping and you'll soon be serving up the perfect Friday night pizza!*

**SERVES 2**
Prepares in 40 minutes, plus rising
Cooks in 40–50 minutes

15 g/½ oz butter
1 tbsp olive oil, plus extra for brushing and drizzling
1 small onion, finely chopped
1 garlic clove, finely chopped
½ celery stick, finely chopped
200 g/7 oz canned chopped tomatoes
1 tbsp tomato purée
brown sugar, to taste
1 tbsp chopped fresh basil
3 tbsp water
140 g/5 oz mozzarella cheese, sliced
4 tomatoes, sliced

1 fresh basil sprig
2 tbsp grated Parmesan cheese
salt and pepper

## Pizza Dough

225 g/8 oz strong white flour, plus extra for dusting
1 tsp salt
½ tsp easy-blend dried yeast
1 tbsp olive oil, plus extra for oiling
150 ml/5 fl oz lukewarm water

1. To make the dough, sift the flour and salt into a bowl and stir in the yeast. Make a well in the centre and pour in the oil and water, then mix to a soft dough. Knead for 10 minutes on a lightly floured surface. Shape into a ball, place in an oiled plastic bag and leave to rise in a warm place for 1 hour, or until doubled.

2. Melt the butter with the oil in a saucepan. Add the onion, garlic and celery and cook over a low heat, stirring occasionally, for 5 minutes, until softened. Stir in the canned tomatoes, tomato purée, sugar to taste, chopped basil and water and season to taste with salt and pepper. Increase the heat to medium and bring to the boil, then reduce the heat and simmer, stirring occasionally, for 15–20 minutes, or until thickened. Remove from the heat and set aside.

3. Preheat the oven to 220°C/425°F/ Gas Mark 7. Brush a baking sheet with oil. Knock back the dough and knead briefly on a lightly floured surface. Roll out into a round and transfer to the prepared baking sheet. Push up a rim all the way around.

4. Spread the tomato sauce evenly over the base. Arrange the mozzarella and tomato slices alternately on top. Coarsely tear the basil leaves and put them on the pizza, then sprinkle with the Parmesan. Drizzle with the oil and bake in the preheated oven for 15–20 minutes, or until crisp and golden. Serve the pizza immediately.

# Lamb-cumin Pitta Burgers with Tahini Sauce

*Lightly toast, then grind, whole cumin seeds to add the finest spice flavour to these tempting lamb burgers, and use individual round pitta breads instead of halving larger oval ones, for extra appeal too.*

**SERVES 6**
Prepares in 20–25 minutes
Cooks in 10–14 minutes

450 g/1 lb fresh lamb mince
3 tbsp finely chopped red onion
1 tbsp chopped fresh coriander, plus
 extra leaves to garnish
1 tsp salt
½ tsp pepper
½ tsp ground cumin
3 large pitta breads, warmed,
 halved and split
tomato slices
cucumber slices
olive oil, for drizzling
salt and pepper

## Tahini Sauce
90 ml/3 fl oz tahini
90 ml/3 fl oz natural yogurt
1 garlic clove, finely chopped

1. Preheat the grill to high. Place the lamb in a bowl and add the onion, coriander, salt, pepper and the cumin, then gently mix until thoroughly combined.

2. Divide the mixture into six equal-sized portions, form each portion into a 7.5-cm/3-inch wide patty and place in a grill pan lined with foil.

3. Place the grill pan under the preheated grill and cook the patties for about 5–7 minutes on each side, or until cooked through and browned.

4. To make the tahini sauce, put the tahini, yogurt and garlic into a bowl. Season to taste with salt and pepper and mix to combine.

5. Stuff the burgers into the pitta halves, then drizzle with the tahini sauce. Add the tomato and cucumber slices and the coriander leaves, drizzle with the oil and serve immediately.

# Chicken Chow Mein

Transport your taste buds to China and create this ever-popular takeaway dish in the comfort of your own kitchen. Taking just a matter of minutes to prepare and cook, it's the ideal fodder for a Friday night.

**SERVES 4**
Prepares in 15 minutes
Cooks in 17 minutes

250 g/9 oz dried medium Chinese egg noodles
2 tbsp sunflower oil
280 g/10 oz cooked chicken breasts, shredded
1 garlic clove, finely chopped
1 red pepper, thinly sliced
100 g/3½ oz shiitake mushrooms, sliced
6 spring onions, sliced
100 g/3½ oz beansprouts
3 tbsp soy sauce
1 tbsp sesame oil

1. Cook the noodles as per the packet instructions. Drain well and set aside.

2. Heat a wok over a medium heat, then add the oil. Add the shredded chicken, garlic, red pepper, mushrooms, spring onions and beansprouts to the wok and stir-fry for about 5 minutes.

3. Add the noodles to the wok, toss well and stir-fry for a further 5 minutes. Drizzle over the soy sauce and sesame oil and toss until thoroughly combined. Transfer to warmed bowls and serve immediately.

# Thai Green Chicken Curry & Udon Noodles

*Rustled up in less than an hour, this truly authentic Thai green curry is bursting with fresh flavours and vibrant green garden herbs. Serve with a refreshingly crisp cucumber salad for a truly tasty meal.*

**SERVES 4**
Prepares in 20–25 minutes, plus cooling
Cooks in 25–28 minutes

*1 tbsp vegetable oil*
*1 shallot, diced*
*1–3 tsp Thai green curry paste*
*425 ml/15 fl oz canned coconut milk*
*1 tbsp Thai fish sauce*
*juice of 1 lime*
*1 tbsp soft light brown sugar*

*25 g/1 oz fresh basil leaves*
*25 g/1 oz fresh coriander leaves*
*450 g/1 lb fresh udon noodles*
*350 g/12 oz cooked chicken, shredded*
*3 spring onions, thinly sliced, to garnish*

1. Heat the oil in a non-stick frying pan over a medium heat. Add the shallot and cook for 5 minutes until soft. Add the curry paste and cook, stirring, for 1 minute.

2. Open the can of coconut milk and scoop off the thick cream that will have risen to the top. Add the coconut cream to the pan with the fish sauce, lime juice and sugar. Cook, stirring frequently, for 1–2 minutes.

3. Stir in the remaining coconut milk and bring the mixture to the boil. Reduce the heat to low and simmer, stirring occasionally, for a further 5 minutes, or until the sauce thickens. Remove from the heat and leave to cool slightly.

4. Transfer the mixture to a food processor, add the basil and coriander and process until smooth and bright green. Return the sauce to the pan and reheat over a medium–low heat.

5. Cook the noodles according to the packet instructions and place them in a large serving bowl.

6. Add the chicken and sauce to the noodles and toss to combine. Serve immediately, garnished with the spring onions.

# Bengali Vegetable Curry

An aromatic mixed vegetable curry, served simply with some perfect fluffy rice, creates this standout vegetarian dish that is ideal for enjoying at the end of a busy working week.

SERVES 2
Prepares in 20–25 minutes, plus soaking
Cooks in 28–35 minutes

6 tbsp white poppy seeds (khus khus)
3 tbsp black mustard seeds
2 tsp grated fresh ginger
4 tbsp vegetable or groundnut oil
2 green chillies, split lengthways
1 tbsp panch phoran
200 g/7 oz fresh bittergourd (karela) or
   squash, cut into 1.5-cm/½-inch cubes
2 potatoes, cut into 1.5-cm/½-inch cubes
1 aubergine, cut into 1.5-cm/½-inch cubes
1 courgette, cut into 1.5-cm/½-inch cubes
1 carrot, cut into 1.5-cm/½-inch cubes
1 tomato, finely chopped
100 g/3½ oz fresh or frozen peas
400 ml/14 fl oz cold water
¼ tsp ground turmeric
2 tsp salt
1 tsp palm sugar
125 ml/4 fl oz milk

1. Soak the white poppy seeds and 2 tablespoons of the mustard seeds in a bowl of warm water for 1 hour. Drain the seeds and blend well with the ginger to make a paste.

2. Heat the oil in a large frying pan and add the remaining mustard seeds and the chillies. When the mustard seeds start to pop, add the panch phoran and all the vegetables. Add half of the water and stir to mix well, then cover tightly and cook, stirring frequently, over a medium heat for 10–12 minutes.

3. Add half of the white poppy seed and mustard seed paste, the turmeric and salt. Add the remaining water and cook, stirring frequently, over a low–medium heat for a further 10–15 minutes.

4. Add the remaining white poppy seed and mustard seed paste, the palm sugar and milk and cook for a further 5 minutes, or until the vegetables are tender. Remove the chillies and serve immediately.

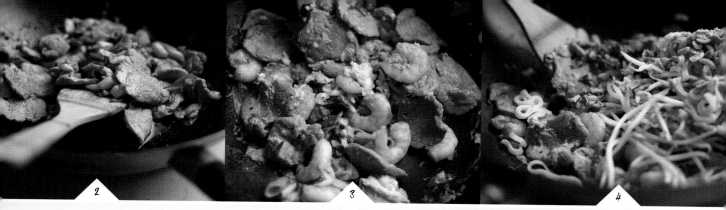

# Pork Pad Thai

This popular Thai pork noodle dish is quick and easy to create at home, making it the ideal choice for a Friday night supper with friends. A wonderful fusion of fresh flavours, it's sure to impress your guests.

**SERVES 4**
Prepares in 20 minutes
Cooks in 15–20 minutes

225 g/8 oz thick dried rice noodles
2 tbsp groundnut or vegetable oil
4 spring onions, roughly chopped
2 garlic cloves, crushed
2 red chillies, deseeded and sliced
225 g/8 oz pork fillet, trimmed
   and thinly sliced
115 g/4 oz cooked peeled large prawns
juice of 1 lime
2 tbsp Thai fish sauce
2 eggs, beaten
55 g/2 oz fresh beansprouts
handful of chopped fresh coriander
55 g/2 oz unsalted peanuts, chopped
lime wedges, to serve (optional)

1. Prepare the noodles according to the packet instructions. Drain and set aside.

2. Heat a wok over a medium–high heat, then add the oil. Add the spring onions, garlic and chillies and stir-fry for 1–2 minutes. Add the pork and stir-fry over a high heat for 1–2 minutes, or until the pork is completely cooked through.

3. Add the prawns, lime juice, fish sauce and eggs and stir-fry over a medium heat for 2–3 minutes until the eggs have set and the prawns are heated through.

4. Add the beansprouts, most of the coriander, the peanuts and the noodles and stir-fry for 30 seconds until heated through. Garnish with the remaining coriander and serve immediately with lime wedges, if desired.

# Hot & Spicy Ketchup

### MAKES ABOUT 600 ML/ 1 PINT
Prepares in 15 minutes
Cooks in 2½ hours

2.25 kg/5 lb tomatoes, chopped

2 red jalapeño chillies, chopped

1 sweet white onion, roughly chopped

1 tsp salt, plus extra to taste

1 tsp fennel seeds

1 tsp black mustard seeds

250 ml/9 fl oz cider vinegar

100 g/3½ oz soft light brown sugar

1 cinnamon stick

½ tsp ground nutmeg

½ tsp sweet paprika

1–3 tsp cayenne pepper

pepper

1. Put the tomatoes, chillies, onion and salt into a large saucepan over a high heat. Stir until the tomatoes begin to break down, then reduce the heat to low, cover and simmer for 30 minutes, or until the tomatoes are pulpy.

2. Meanwhile, put the fennel seeds and mustard seeds on a square of muslin, bring together the sides and tie to make a bag, then set aside.

3. Pass the tomato mixture through a sieve into a large saucepan, rubbing backwards and forwards with a wooden spoon and scraping the base of the sieve to produce as much purée as possible.

4. Add the spice bag and the vinegar, sugar, cinnamon stick, nutmeg, paprika and cayenne pepper. Season to taste with pepper, then stir until the sugar dissolves. Bring to the boil, then reduce the heat and simmer, uncovered, for 1½ hours, skimming the surface as necessary, until the sauce is reduced and thickened.

5. Remove the spice bag and the cinnamon stick. Transfer to a bowl and leave to cool completely.

6. The ketchup can be used immediately, or stored in an airtight container in the refrigerator for up to 1 month.

# Sweet Chilli Sauce

**MAKES ABOUT 150 ML/
5 FL OZ**
Prepares in 15 minutes
Cooks in 25 minutes

4 red jalapeño chillies, halved
2 large garlic cloves,
roughly chopped
4-cm/1½-inch piece fresh ginger,
roughly chopped
150 ml/5 fl oz rice wine or
cider vinegar
150 g/5½ oz caster sugar
150 ml/5 fl oz water
2 tbsp dried chilli flakes
¼ tsp salt

1. Put the chillies, garlic and ginger into a small food processor and pulse until finely chopped but not puréed, scraping down the sides as necessary. Alternatively, finely chop the chillies, garlic and ginger with a sharp knife.

2. Add the vinegar, sugar and water and blend together.

3. Transfer the ingredients to a heavy-based saucepan over a high heat. Add the chilli flakes and salt, stirring to dissolve the sugar.

4. Bring to the boil, without stirring. Reduce the heat to medium–low and simmer, stirring frequently so the sauce doesn't stick to the base of the pan, for about 20 minutes, or until thickened.

5. Transfer the sauce to a bowl and leave to cool completely, stirring occasionally. The sauce can be used immediately, or stored in an airtight container in the refrigerator for up to 2 weeks.

# Chipotle Pork Fajitas

*These fabulous fajitas are great for sharing with a small gathering of friends. Once all the different elements are prepared and cooked, everyone can simply assemble their own fajitas and get stuck in.*

**SERVES 4**
Prepares in 25 minutes
Cooks in 20–25 minutes

1 tbsp ground chipotle chilli
2 tsp soft light brown sugar
1 tsp salt
1 tsp ground cumin
1 tsp dried oregano
½ tsp garlic powder
1 pork fillet,
   cut into 1-cm/½-inch strips
2 bacon rashers, diced
1 tbsp olive oil
1 onion, sliced
1 red pepper, chopped
1 yellow pepper, chopped
1 tbsp garlic purée

### To Serve
8–12 flour tortillas
salsa
guacamole or sliced avocado
soured cream
coriander sprigs
lime halves, for squeezing

1. Preheat the oven to 200°C/400°F/Gas Mark 6.

2. Combine the ground chilli, sugar, salt, cumin, oregano and garlic powder in a small bowl.

3. Place the pork and bacon pieces into a large bowl with the spice mixture and toss until the meat is thoroughly coated in the spice mixture.

4. Heat the oil in a large frying pan over a medium–high heat. Add the pork and bacon (you may have to cook the meat in two batches to avoid crowding) and cook, stirring, for 4–5 minutes until the meat is browned. Transfer to a plate.

5. Add the onion, red pepper and yellow pepper, and the garlic purée to the frying pan and cook for about 4 minutes, or until the vegetables begin to soften. Return the meat to the pan and fry until warmed and cooked through.

6. Meanwhile, wrap the tortillas in foil and place in the preheated oven to warm for 5 minutes.

7. Serve the pork mixture in a bowl alongside the warmed tortillas, salsa, guacamole, soured cream, coriander sprigs and lime halves. Assemble the fajitas and eat while hot.

# Colossal Lamb Kebab with Hot Chilli Sauce

Griddled spicy lamb pieces are
served on a warm flatbread
and topped with hot chilli
sauce and yogurt to create this
tantalizing Friday night supper,
ideal for one mighty appetite,
but even better for two sharing.

**MAKES 1**
Prepares in 20 minutes
Cooks in 9–11 minutes

500 g/1 lb 2 oz leg of lamb, diced
2 tbsp olive oil
1 tsp dried thyme
1 tsp paprika
1 tsp ground cumin
1 large flatbread
1 small red onion, sliced
1 tomato, chopped
small bunch fresh coriander, chopped
½ lemon
salt and pepper
sriracha or other hot chilli sauce
   and natural yogurt, to serve

1. Place the lamb with the olive oil,
thyme and spices in a medium bowl.
Season to taste with salt and pepper
and mix thoroughly to combine.

2. Preheat a large griddle pan or
a barbecue.

3. Thread the lamb pieces onto
two large skewers, and cook
in the preheated pan or on the
barbecue for 4–5 minutes on each
side, or until cooked through.

4. Heat a large, dry frying pan
and cook the flatbread for a few
seconds on both sides until soft.

5. Remove the lamb from the
skewers, place on the flatbread
and top with the onion, tomato
and coriander. Squeeze over the
lemon and serve immediately
with the sriracha and natural
yogurt drizzled over the top.

# Blazing Hot Wings with Blue Cheese Dressing

*If you are feeling weary after a hectic week at work, wake up your taste buds with these sizzling hot and spicy grilled chicken wings accompanied by a creamy blue cheese dressing. They are finger-licking good!*

**SERVES 4**
Prepares in 30 minutes,
 plus marinating
Cooks in 30–35 minutes

4 tbsp maple syrup
1 tbsp hot pepper sauce
24 chicken wings, wingtips removed
 and each wing cut into two pieces
 at the 'elbow' joint
sunflower oil, for brushing
salt and pepper

## Blue Cheese Dressing

125 g/4½ oz blue cheese
1 tbsp English mustard
300 ml/10 fl oz soured cream
2 tbsp finely snipped fresh chives
salt and pepper

1. Combine the maple syrup and hot pepper sauce in a large bowl. Season to taste with salt and pepper.

2. Add the chicken wings to the bowl and rub the wings into the sauce mixture. Set aside at room temperature for 30 minutes. If making in advance, cover the bowl with clingfilm and chill in the refrigerator until 30 minutes before cooking.

3. When ready to grill, preheat the grill to high. Line the grill tray with foil, shiny-side up, and brush the rack with oil.

4. Arrange the chicken wing pieces on the grill rack, fleshy-side down. Position the rack 13 cm/5 inches away from the heat and cook for 20 minutes, basting occasionally with any marinade left in the bowl.

5. Turn the chicken pieces over, baste and continue to cook for 10–15 minutes, or until the skin is dark golden brown and the juices run clear when the thickest part of the meat is pierced with a sharp knife.

6. Meanwhile, to make the dressing, blend the cheese, mustard and soured cream in a food processor. Stir in the chives and season to taste.

7. Serve the chicken wings hot, with the dressing on the side.

# Savvy Storecupboard Ingredients

*It's a good idea to keep a decent stock of storecupboard essentials, the type of ingredients that you use regularly in cooking. They will help to supply savvy solutions for putting together tasty meals after a hard week at work. Storecupboard spices in particular provide an easy and effective way to add maximum flavour to basic dishes with minimum effort, allowing you more time to unwind and relax on a Friday night.*

There is a vast variety of spices available, so choose them carefully and keep a small supply of spices that you use regularly in the cupboard, plus a modest selection of dried herbs too. Popular dried spices ideal for the storecupboard include: allspice, caraway seeds, cardamom pods, cayenne, chilli, cinnamon, cloves, coriander, cumin, curry paste or powder, fennel seeds, fenugreek seeds, garam masala, ginger, mixed spice, mustard seeds, nutmeg, paprika, smoked paprika, star anise, sumac and turmeric. Dried herbs that are great as storecupboard stand-bys include: bay leaves, bouquet garni, marjoram, mixed herbs, oregano, rosemary, sage, tarragon and thyme.

To maximize the finest flavour from spices, buy good quality whole spices and grind them yourself, using a clean electric coffee grinder (kept specifically for spices) or a spice grinder. Alternatively, you can use a pestle and mortar for grinding but you'll need a bit more elbow grease for this! It's best to buy whole spices in relatively small quantities as they will gradually lose their flavour and become stale, and make sure you grind them fresh each time. If you do use ready-ground spices, be sure to keep them in airtight containers or jars in a cool, dark, dry place, and replace them every 6 months or so, as they lose their fresh flavour quite quickly – the same applies to dried herbs too.

Dry-frying whole spices in a heavy-based frying pan for a few minutes, or until they release their delicious fragrances, before grinding them will also bring out their full aromatic flavour and vastly improve the taste of your dishes.

Indian and Chinese supermarkets are a great source for both fresh and dried spices and herbs, but nowadays many supermarkets or small shops stock a wide range too, as do many delis and specialist online suppliers.

Ready-made dried spice blends or herb mixes are handy to have in case you don't have time to make them from scratch. These include: Cajun, Chinese five-spice powder, Creole, dukkah, fajita, herbes de Provence, Italian mixed herbs, Jamaican jerk, piri piri, ras-el-hanout, Thai seven-spice powder and za'atar. Gourmet spice rubs and pastes are also great go-to flavour improvers if you are short of time.

It is useful to have some essential storecupboard staples in the cupboard at all times, so you can create dishes in no time at all. It's worth keeping a stocklist of these so you know if you need to replace any when you go shopping.

These essentials include: canned tomatoes, sweetcorn and beans; canned fish; condiments such as chilli sauce, soy sauce, tomato purée, sun-dried tomato paste, pesto, passata, smooth and grainy mustards, Worcestershire sauce, Thai fish sauce and mayonnaise; a selection of dried beans, pasta, rice, grains and lentils, including on-trend grains and seeds such as polenta, farro, spelt and quinoa; sun-dried tomatoes; olives; bottled grilled red peppers and artichokes; good quality bouillon powder; tahini; a small selection of different oils and vinegars; a selection of dried fruit, nuts, seeds and pine nuts; sugars; and flours.

It's also a good idea to have some superior storecupboard ingredients to hand for more elaborate dishes or guests.

These might include: cold-pressed oils; quality balsamic vinegar; Kalamata olives; arborio risotto rice; Puy lentils; quality sea salt flakes; harissa paste; nut oils for dressings; green peppercorns in brine; Sichuan peppercorns; capers or caper berries; juniper berries; saffron; tamarind paste; anchovies; dried ceps; preserved truffles; pickled lemons; wasabi paste; vanilla pods; almond extract; orange flower water and rose water; maple syrup; stem ginger; and good quality dark chocolate.

# Chipotle Ketchup & Chipotle Mustard

*Add some zing and spice to mealtimes with these two simple but sensational sides, perfect for serving with grilled or barbecued steaks, kebabs, burgers or sausages or chargrilled vegetables.*

**SERVES 8**
Prepares in 15 minutes,
 plus cooling and chilling
Cooks in 5 minutes

## Chipotle Ketchup

*225 ml/8 fl oz tomato ketchup*
*½ tsp Worcestershire sauce*
*½ tsp light brown sugar*
*1 tbsp fresh lemon juice, or to taste*
*1½ tsp chipotle powder, or to taste*
*1 tsp ground cumin*
*½ tsp ground turmeric*
*¼ tsp ground ginger*
*salt*

## Chipotle Mustard

*125 ml/4 fl oz Dijon mustard*
*1 tsp chipotle powder, or to taste*

1. To make the ketchup, combine all of the ketchup ingredients, with salt to taste, in a small saucepan and place over a medium heat. Bring to a simmer and cook, stirring frequently, for 5 minutes, or until the ketchup is slightly thickened.

2. Remove the saucepan from the heat and leave to cool. Transfer the ketchup to a sterilized jar, cover, and refrigerate until ready to use.

3. To make the chipotle mustard, place the ingredients in a small bowl and stir to thoroughly combine. Transfer to a sterilized jar, cover, and refrigerate until ready to use.

# Rosemary, Sea Salt & Sesame Popcorn

SERVES 4

Prepares in 10–15 minutes

Cooks in 6–8 minutes

40 g/1½ oz sesame seeds

2 tbsp olive oil

2 rosemary stems

200 g/7 oz popping corn

1 tsp sea salt

2 tbsp balsamic vinegar

1. Add the sesame seeds to a large frying pan with 1 teaspoon of the oil, cover and cook over a medium heat for 2–3 minutes, shaking the pan from time to time, until the seeds are toasted golden brown and beginning to pop. Scoop out of the pan into a bowl and wipe out the pan with a piece of kitchen paper.

2. Tear the rosemary into large pieces and add the remaining oil and the rosemary to the pan. Heat gently, shaking the pan to release the rosemary's oil. Add the corn, cover with the lid and cook over a medium heat for 3–4 minutes, shaking the pan, until all the popcorn has popped.

3. Remove from the heat and sprinkle with the toasted sesame seeds and season with the salt and vinegar, then tip into a serving bowl, discarding the rosemary just before eating.

# Root Vegetable Crisps with Herby Yogurt Dip

**SERVES 4**

Prepares in 30–35 minutes, plus chilling and cooling

Cooks in 12–16 minutes

*1 kg/2 lb 4 oz mixed root vegetables, such as carrots, parsnips, sweet potatoes or golden beetroot, very thinly sliced*

*4 tbsp virgin olive oil*

*sea salt and pepper*

## Herby Yogurt Dip

*200 g/7 oz Greek-style natural yogurt*

*2 garlic cloves, finely chopped*

*4 tbsp finely chopped fresh herbs, such as flat-leaf parsley, chives, basil or oregano*

1. Preheat the oven to 200°C/400°F/ Gas Mark 6. To make the herby yogurt dip, spoon the yogurt into a small bowl, then stir in the garlic and herbs, and season with salt and pepper. Cover and chill in the refrigerator until ready to serve.

2. Put the vegetables in a large bowl. Slowly drizzle over the oil, gently turning the vegetables as you go, until they are thoroughly coated.

3. Arrange the vegetables over three baking sheets in a single layer, then season with salt and pepper. Bake for 8–10 minutes, then check the crisps – the slices in the corners of the trays will cook more quickly, so transfer any that are crisp and golden to a wire rack. Cook the rest for 2–3 minutes more, then transfer any more cooked crisps to the wire rack. Cook the remaining slices for 2–3 minutes more if needed, then transfer any remaining crisps to the wire rack and leave to cool.

4. Arrange the crisps in a bowl and spoon the dip into a smaller bowl to serve.

# Saturday Kickstart

## Breakfasts & Lunches

---

*Whether you are an early riser who likes to power up for the day with an early morning work-out or you prefer a more leisurely lie-in, Saturday morning should be all about preparing for the rest of the weekend. This is the time to plan for the fun ahead and, if you haven't already done so, spend some time deciding what to cook and sourcing fresh ingredients, allowing yourself time to indulge your passion for creative cooking.*

---

*On a Saturday morning, give yourself plenty of time to plan and get ahead, so you are relaxed and ready to create a fabulous feast and enjoy an evening of entertaining friends or family. Prepare make-ahead dishes to serve later if you can, like soup, pâté, ice cream or sorbet, or why not bake some fresh bread for lunch or to accompany your evening meal?*

All the recipes in this chapter will either help you to kickstart the day with a leisurely breakfast, or relish a relaxing lunch a bit later, while enjoying the good company of those around you.

If your focus first thing is on fitness and you enjoy a Saturday morning work-out, or perhaps you regularly go out for a run, cycle or gym session, boost your energy levels before you go with one of our sensational Single Shot Juice Boosters or Beetroot Power Juice. You'll be off and running before you know it!

If you're more inclined to take things a little easier first thing, then we include an appealing collection of breakfast recipes to get you going. Choose from classics like Creamy Porridge with Blackberries or Cranberry & Seed Muesli, or for something a bit more substantial, there are ever-popular picks, such as The Best Bacon Butty or Croque Monsieur, to start your day off perfectly.

If you prefer something sweet to accompany your morning mug of tea or coffee, then you could munch your way through some warm Coffee & Pecan Mini Breakfast Muffins, or if you have guests staying over, the Coconut Flour Pancakes will go down a treat.

As lunch beckons a bit later on and perhaps friends or family have joined you, tempt their taste buds with favourites like Fish Finger Sandwiches, Turkey Wraps with Avocado Salsa or simple but sophisticated Smoked Salmon Bagels. For vegetable lovers, Pea Soup with Blue Cheese & Croûtons or Flatbread Pizzas with

Courgette Ribbons are bound to appeal. If you fancy trying a different type of grain, why not opt for the tempting Green Farro Salad with Feta?

Now is a good time to decide where you are eating your meal tonight and take time to set the table in readiness for your guests arriving later. If it looks set to be a balmy summer's day, then perhaps plan to eat al fresco later and make sure the garden furniture is all set up and ready to use. On the other hand, if the weather has turned wet or wintry and there's a distinct dampness or chill in the air, stock up the wood store and get the wood burner or open fire ready to roar.

# Greek-style Yogurt with Orange Zest & Toasted Seeds

**SERVES 2**

Prepares in 10 minutes,
plus cooling

Cooks in 2–3 minutes

2 tsp linseeds
2 tsp pumpkin seeds
2 tsp chia seeds
200 g/7 oz Greek-style natural yogurt
grated zest of 1 small orange,
plus 1 tsp juice

1. Place a small frying pan over a medium heat. When it is hot, tip in the linseeds, pumpkin and chia seeds. Toast, stirring constantly with a wooden spoon, until they start to turn brown and release a nutty aroma. Tip them onto a plate and leave to cool.

2. Spoon the yogurt into two glass pots or serving bowls, then scatter the seeds on top, followed by the orange zest. Sprinkle over the orange juice and serve immediately.

# Creamy Porridge with Blackberries

### SERVES 2

Prepares in 10–12 minutes
Cooks in 10 minutes

100 g/3½ oz large rolled oats
small pinch of sea salt
600 ml/1 pint cold water
3½ tbsp double cream
1 tbsp stevia

### To Serve

1 tbsp pumpkin seeds
6 large blackberries, quartered
double cream, for pouring

1. Put the oats and salt in a medium saucepan and pour over the water. Bring to the boil, then reduce the heat to medium–low and simmer, stirring regularly, for 5–6 minutes, or until the oats are thick but have a dense pouring consistency.

2. Stir in the cream and stevia. Spoon the porridge into two bowls, top with the pumpkin seeds and blackberries, and serve immediately with a little extra cream for pouring over.

# Coffee & Pecan Mini Breakfast Muffins

**MAKES 9**

Prepares in 25 minutes, plus cooling

Cooks in 20 minutes

50 g/1¾ oz coconut flour

¼ tsp baking powder

½ tsp bicarbonate of soda

1 tbsp stevia

30 g/1 oz pecan nuts, roughly chopped

150 ml/5 fl oz soured cream

5 tbsp vegetable oil

2 large eggs, beaten

5 tbsp prepared espresso or strong instant coffee

1 tsp rice malt syrup

salt

1. Preheat the oven to 160°C/325°F/ Gas Mark 3. Put 9 mini muffin cases into a mini muffin tray.

2. Put the flour, baking powder, bicarbonate of soda, stevia, 20 g/ ¾ oz pecan nuts and a small pinch of salt in a large bowl and mix well. Add the soured cream, oil, eggs and 4 tablespoons of espresso, and stir until evenly mixed. Leave to stand for a moment, then spoon the mixture into the mini muffin cases.

3. Bake in the preheated oven for 20 minutes, or until well risen and the tops spring back when pressed with a fingertip. Leave to cool slightly, then transfer to a wire rack.

4. To make the topping, put the syrup and remaining 1 tablespoon of espresso in a bowl and mix. Spoon a small drizzle over each muffin. Sprinkle on the remaining 10 g/¼ oz pecan nuts and serve warm, or store in an airtight container for up to 2 days.

# Cranberry & Seed Muesli

### SERVES 6

Prepares in 20 minutes, plus
soaking or chilling

No cooking

*175 g/6 oz porridge oats*
*60 g/2¼ oz rye flakes*
*75 g/2¾ oz unblanched almonds,*
*roughly chopped*
*50 g/1¾ oz dried cranberries*
*2 tbsp sunflower seeds*
*2 tbsp pumpkin seeds*
*2 tbsp linseeds*
*2 crisp dessert apples, cored and*
*coarsely grated*
*400 ml/14 fl oz fresh*
*apple juice, plus extra to serve*

1. Put the oats, rye flakes,
almonds, cranberries, sunflower
seeds, pumpkin seeds and
linseeds in a large bowl and
mix well. Stir in the apples.

2. Add the apple juice, stir, cover
and leave to soak for 1 hour, or
chill in the refrigerator overnight.

3. Spoon the mixture into six serving
bowls. Serve with a small jug of extra
fresh apple juice for pouring over.

# Single Shot Juice Boosters

### SERVES 1
Each prepares in 5 minutes
No cooking

#### Beetroot Booster
*2 beetroots, halved*
*4 tbsp chilled water (optional)*

#### Kiwi Fruit Booster
*2 kiwi fruits*

#### Blueberry Booster
*150 g/5½ oz blueberries*
*4 tbsp chilled water*

1. For the Beetroot Booster, feed the beetroot through a juicer. Pour into a glass, top up with the water (if using) and serve.

2. For the Kiwi Fruit Booster, feed the kiwi fruits through a juicer. Pour into a glass and serve.

3. For the Blueberry Booster, put the blueberries and water in a blender, then whizz until smooth. Pour into a glass and serve.

# Beetroot Power Juice

### SERVES 1
Prepares in 10 minutes
No cooking

*2 beetroots, halved*
*30 g/1 oz linseeds*
*4 plums, quartered and pitted*
*150 g/5½ oz seedless red grapes*
*225 ml/8 fl oz chilled water*
*ice, to serve (optional)*

1. Feed the beetroots through a juicer. Put the linseeds into a blender and whizz until finely ground.

2. Add the beetroot juice, plums, grapes and water to the blender and whizz until smooth.

3. Pour the juice into a glass, add ice (if using) and serve immediately.

# Coconut Flour Pancakes with Lemon Drizzle

*These tasty pancakes made with coconut milk and coconut flour (and cooked in coconut oil!) will go down a treat with any guests. The lemon drizzle, along with a dollop of crème fraîche, finishes them off perfectly.*

**SERVES 4**
Prepares in 25–30 minutes
Cooks in 18 minutes

2 large eggs
100 ml/3½ fl oz coconut milk
125 ml/4 fl oz cold water
1 tsp vanilla extract
1 tbsp stevia
50 g/1¾ oz coconut flour
1 tsp bicarbonate of soda
1 tbsp coconut oil
salt
4 tbsp crème fraîche, to serve (optional)

## Lemon Drizzle

finely grated zest and juice of 1 lemon
2 tsp rice malt syrup

1. Crack the eggs into a bowl, then add the coconut milk, water, vanilla, stevia, flour and bicarbonate of soda and season with a pinch of salt. Whisk to a smooth batter, then leave to rest for a moment.

2. Meanwhile, to make the lemon drizzle, put the lemon zest and juice and rice malt syrup in a small bowl and mix well.

3. Heat the coconut oil in a large frying pan over a medium heat. Pour in a tablespoon of the batter, leave to settle for a moment, then add more tablespoons, allowing a little space between each one.

4. Fry for 2 minutes, or until the bottom of each pancake is light brown and the sides are set. Carefully flip over the pancakes using a fish slice and cook for a further 2 minutes.

5. Transfer the pancakes to warm serving plates. Cook the remaining pancakes in the same way. Top each plate of pancakes with a tablespoon of crème fraîche, if using, and spoon over the lemon drizzle.

# Huevos Rancheros

*Create this popular and very tasty Mexican breakfast dish at home with easy-to-source ingredients. It's an ideal hassle-free Saturday morning breakfast for two, good served on its own or with some warm fresh crusty bread.*

**SERVES 2**
Prepares in 15 minutes
Cooks in 25 minutes

2 tbsp olive oil
1 large onion, finely chopped
2 green or red peppers,
  roughly chopped
1 garlic clove, finely chopped
½ tsp dried chilli flakes
4 plum tomatoes, peeled
  and roughly chopped
2 eggs
salt and pepper

1. Heat the oil in a large non-stick frying pan. Add the onion and cook until golden. Add the peppers, garlic and chilli flakes and cook until the peppers are soft.

2. Stir in the tomatoes and season to taste with salt and pepper. Place over a low heat and simmer for 10 minutes.

3. Using the back of a spoon, make two depressions in the mixture in the frying pan. Break the eggs into the depressions, season and cover and cook for 3–4 minutes, or until the eggs are set. Serve immediately.

# The Best Bacon Butty

*Crusty French bread, spread with mayo and stuffed full of crispy smoked bacon, then topped with fried eggs, melting Swiss cheese and chipotle chilli sauce. What better way can there be to kickstart the weekend?*

## MAKES 2
Prepares in 15–20 minutes
Cooks in 8–12 minutes

1 large French stick
4 tbsp mayonnaise
500 g/1 lb 2 oz smoked streaky bacon
4 tbsp vegetable oil
4 eggs
10 Swiss cheese slices
chipotle chilli sauce, to taste

1. Preheat the grill to high.

2. Cut the French stick in half lengthways. Spread the insides of the bread with the mayonnaise and set the French stick aside.

3. Place the bacon on a grill pan and cook under the preheated grill on both sides until crispy or cooked to your liking. Set aside in a warm place.

4. In a frying pan, heat the oil over a medium–low heat. Once hot, crack the eggs gently into the pan, one at a time. Cook the eggs until set, or to your liking.

5. Place the cheese slices on one half of the French stick and top with the bacon, fried eggs and chipotle chilli sauce.

6. Press the two halves of the French stick together gently. Cut in half and serve immediately.

# Croque Monsieur Sandwich

SERVES 1
Prepares in 15 minutes
Cooks in 5–7 minutes

*2 slices white bread, buttered*
*2 slices smoked ham*
*55 g/2 oz Gruyère cheese, grated*
*knob of butter, melted*
*salt and pepper*
*lightly dressed mixed green salad,*
*to serve*

1. Preheat the grill to high.

2. Lay one piece of bread buttered-side up and place the ham on top. Cover with two thirds of the cheese and season. Lay the other slice of bread on top, buttered-side down. Brush the top side with the melted butter and place the sandwich, buttered-side up, under the grill.

3. Grill until browned, then take out from under the grill. Turn the sandwich over and scatter the remaining cheese on top. Replace under the grill and cook until the cheese is bubbling and browned. Remove and serve with a green salad.

# Pea Soup with Blue Cheese & Croûtons

**SERVES 4**

Prepares in 25 minutes
Cooks in 30–35 minutes

40 g/1½ oz unsalted butter
2 shallots, finely chopped
1 litre/1¾ pints vegetable stock
400 g/14 oz podded peas
60 g/2¼ oz crème fraîche
salt and pepper
85 g/3 oz blue cheese,
such as Roquefort,
crumbled, to serve

### Croûtons

2 slices wholemeal
bread, cut into cubes
2 tbsp virgin olive oil

1. To make the croûtons, preheat the oven to 150°C/300°F/Gas Mark 2. Toss the bread cubes with the oil and sprinkle with ½ teaspoon of salt and ½ teaspoon of pepper. Arrange the cubes on a baking sheet in a single layer, then bake in the preheated oven for 25 minutes.

2. Meanwhile, to make the soup, melt the butter in a large saucepan over a medium heat. Add the shallots and fry, stirring, for 2–3 minutes, or until soft. Add the stock and peas, season with salt and pepper, then bring to the boil. Simmer for 15–20 minutes, or until the peas are very tender.

3. Strain the peas through a sieve and reserve the cooking liquid. Transfer the peas to a food processor or blender and process into a purée, then return the mixture to the pan. Gradually stir in the cooking liquid until you have your desired consistency.

4. Reheat the soup. Stir in the crème fraîche and adjust the seasoning. Serve immediately, with the croûtons and blue cheese sprinkled over.

# Flatbread Pizzas with Courgette Ribbons

These flatbread pizzas topped with courgette ribbons, cherry tomatoes and blobs of ricotta cheese will be a firm favourite with vegetarians. Great for a light lunch with a simple side of salad leaves and a glass of something chilled.

SERVES 2
Prepares in 30 minutes
Cooks in 7–10 minutes

50 g/1¾ oz crème fraîche
150 g/5½ oz courgettes, shredded
  into ribbons using a vegetable peeler
55 g/2 oz cherry tomatoes, quartered
50 g/1¾ oz ricotta cheese
1 garlic clove, crushed
2 tbsp olive oil
green salad leaves, to serve (optional)

## Pizza Bases

100 g/3½ oz wholemeal flour,
  plus extra for dusting
50 g/1¾ oz quinoa flour
¾ tsp bicarbonate of soda
1 tbsp olive oil
2 tbsp warm water
salt

1. Preheat the oven to 200°C/400°F/ Gas Mark 6. To make the pizza bases, put the flours and bicarbonate of soda in a mixing bowl, season with salt and stir. Add the oil, then gradually mix in enough of the warm water to make a soft but not sticky dough.

2. Lightly dust a work surface with flour. Knead the dough on the surface for 2 minutes, or until smooth and slightly elastic.

3. Put two large, flat baking sheets in the oven to get hot.

4. Divide the dough into two pieces. Roll out each piece to a circle about 5 mm/¼ inch thick. Remove the hot baking sheets from the oven and, working quickly, lay the dough on top.

5. Spread the crème fraîche over the dough, then sprinkle with the courgettes and tomatoes. Blob the ricotta cheese in small dollops on top.

6. Bake the pizzas for 7–10 minutes, or until the crust is crispy and slightly puffed up, and the ricotta is tinged golden.

7. Mix the garlic and oil together in a jug, and drizzle over the pizzas. Serve with salad leaves, if using.

# Fish Finger Sandwich with Russian Dressing

A simple but tasty lunch, this clever twist on the ever-popular fish finger sandwich, served with a fiery dressing and peppery rocket leaves, is sure to be a top pick with a group of friends.

**MAKES 2**
Prepares in 15 minutes
Cooks in 20 minutes

oil, for deep-frying
20 fish fingers
4 large slices white bread
100 g/3½ oz rocket

## Russian Dressing

2 tbsp mayonnaise
1 tbsp creamed horseradish
1 tbsp tomato ketchup
1 tbsp soured cream
1 tbsp sriracha hot chilli sauce
1 tsp Worcestershire sauce
½ tsp smoked paprika

1. Place enough of the oil for deep-frying into a large, heavy-based saucepan or deep-fat fryer. Heat the oil to 180–190°C/350–375°F, or until a cube of bread browns in 30 seconds.

2. Meanwhile, mix together all of the Russian dressing ingredients in a small bowl and set aside.

3. Deep-fry the fish fingers in batches of ten for 5 minutes or until golden, then remove with a slotted spoon, drain on kitchen paper and leave in a warm place while you cook the remaining fish fingers.

4. Spread some of the dressing on two of the bread slices. Divide the fish fingers between two slices of bread and drizzle over the rest of the dressing. Top with the rocket and the remaining bread slices and serve immediately.

# Smoked Salmon Bagels

Once you have treated yourself and your mates to home-made bagels, you'll never buy shop-bought ones again! Set some time aside in the morning to make these, then enjoy them warm for lunch with smoked salmon and cream cheese.

**MAKES 12**
Prepares in 35–40 minutes, plus standing, rising and cooling
Cooks in 20–25 minutes

1 tbsp easy-blend dried yeast
2 tbsp sugar
3½ tbsp vegetable oil, plus extra for oiling
1 tsp salt
225 ml/8 fl oz warm water
425 g/15 oz plain flour, plus extra for dusting
1 egg, beaten

1 egg, beaten with ¼ tsp salt, for glazing
poppy and sesame seeds, for sprinkling

### Filling
smoked salmon
cream cheese
finely chopped fresh flat-leaf parsley
finely grated lemon zest

1. Combine the yeast and half of the sugar in a small bowl. Heat the remaining sugar, oil, salt and water in a small saucepan for 1–2 minutes, or until warm and the sugar has dissolved. Pour into the yeast mixture, cover with a tea towel and leave to stand for 5–7 minutes, or until the mixture begins to bubble. Put the flour into a food processor and, with the machine running, pour in the yeast mixture, then add the egg and process until a ball of dough forms.

2. Add a little more flour if the dough is sticky – it should be smooth and elastic. Lightly oil a large bowl and add the ball of dough, turning to coat on all sides to prevent a crust from forming. Cover with the tea towel and leave to rise in a warm place for 1½–2 hours, or until the dough has doubled in size. Turn out onto a lightly floured work surface. Knead lightly to deflate.

3. Divide the dough into 12 equal-sized pieces. Roll each into a rope about 18 cm/7 inches long and shape into a ring. Wet one end and press firmly to seal. Arrange on a floured baking tray, cover with the tea towel and leave to rise for 25 minutes, or until doubled in size. Meanwhile, preheat the oven to 200°C/400°F/Gas Mark 6. Lightly oil two large baking trays.

4. Bring a large saucepan of water to the boil. Working in batches, slide a few bagels into the water and cook for 1 minute. Remove with a slotted spoon and drain on paper towels.

5. Arrange the bagels on the baking trays and carefully brush with the egg mixture. Sprinkle half with sesame seeds and the remainder with poppy seeds. Bake for 12–15 minutes, or until golden and shiny. Remove and place on a wire rack to cool slightly. Serve warm with smoked salmon, cream cheese, parsley and lemon zest.

# Turkey Wraps with Avocado Salsa

These tasty turkey wraps are great for sharing, so once the turkey is marinated and the salsa is chopped, warm the tortillas and get grilling, so that everyone can get stuck in and assemble their own wraps.

**SERVES 4**
Prepares in 30 minutes,
  plus marinating
Cooks in 12 minutres

4 thin turkey breast escalopes,
  350 g/12 oz total weight
olive oil, for brushing
4 romaine or cos lettuce leaves,
  thick stems removed, leaves sliced
  into ribbons
4 corn tortillas, warmed
3 tbsp soured cream

## Marinade
juice of 2 oranges
1 tsp cumin seeds, lightly crushed

½ tsp dried red chilli flakes
4 tbsp olive oil
salt and pepper

## Salsa
2 avocados, peeled, stoned,
  and diced
1 small red onion, diced
2 tomatoes, deseeded and diced
2 tbsp chopped fresh coriander
juice of 1 lime

1. Slice the turkey escalopes into 4 x 6-cm/1½ x 2½-inch strips. Place in a shallow dish.

2. To make the marinade, whisk together all the marinade ingredients. Pour over the turkey, cover and marinate in the refrigerator for 4 hours, or overnight. Remove from the refrigerator at least 30 minutes before cooking to bring to room temperature.

3. To make the salsa, combine all the ingredients in a small bowl.

4. Preheat the grill to high. Drain the turkey, discarding the marinade. Thread the strips concertina-style onto metal skewers (or use wooden skewers with aluminium foil wrapped around the ends so that they don't burn) and brush the turkey with oil.

5. Place the skewers on a rack in the grill pan and cook under the preheated grill for about 5 minutes on each side, or until the turkey is cooked through and starting to brown at the edges. Check that the centre of the meat is no longer pink and the juices run clear when the thickest part of the meat is cut through with a knife. Remove the turkey from the skewers, set aside and keep warm.

6. Divide the lettuce between the tortillas and arrange the turkey on top. Add a little soured cream and salsa. Roll the bottoms and sides of the tortillas over the filling and serve immediately.

# Green Farro Salad with Feta

*Try a different grain and make this tempting salad of cooked farro, feta cheese and vibrant green vegetables and herbs, all tossed together with a light lemony dressing.*

**SERVES 4**
Prepares in 25 minutes,
  plus cooling and standing
Cooks in 15 minutes

225 g/8 oz quick-cook farro, rinsed
½ tsp salt
50 g/1¾ oz fresh peas
5 spring onions, some green included,
  thinly sliced
½ courgette, coarsely grated
35 g/1¼ oz baby spinach, shredded
4 tbsp chopped fresh mint leaves
4 tbsp chopped fresh flat-leaf parsley
85 g/3 oz feta cheese, cubed
sumac or paprika, for sprinkling

## Dressing
2 tbsp lemon juice
6 tbsp extra virgin olive oil,
  plus extra for drizzling
salt and pepper

1. Put the farro and salt into a saucepan with water to cover. Bring to the boil, then reduce the heat, cover and simmer for 10 minutes, or until tender but still chewy. Drain, then spread out on a tray to cool slightly. Tip into a serving bowl while still lukewarm.

2. To make the dressing, combine the lemon juice with salt and pepper to taste in a small bowl. Whisk in the oil. Pour over the farro and mix gently.

3. Stir in the peas, spring onions, courgette, spinach, mint and parsley. Leave to stand at room temperature for 30 minutes.

4. Divide the mixture between four plates. Arrange the cheese on top, sprinkle with a little sumac and drizzle with oil. Serve immediately.

# Saturday Evening Specials

*This inspirational chapter features a sensational selection of more elaborate dishes, ideal for entertaining and decadent dining. These recipes will allow you to showcase your finesse and flair in the kitchen and create first-rate dishes for everyone to enjoy. Make Saturday evening special – whether you are having a romantic meal or hosting an evening with friends.*

*As a competent and creative cook, you'll relish the challenge of trying something new, but especially when entertaining, don't try to cook out of your comfort zone or get too daunted by complicated techniques. Don't attempt to make too many dishes, otherwise a Saturday evening special may turn into a Saturday evening meltdown.*

Choose and cook with seasonal ingredients if you can, as the taste will be so much better. Select dishes that reflect the time of year too – choose warming, comforting dishes for chilly, wintry evenings and lighter, refreshing dishes for warm summer evenings. If you can prepare the starter or dessert ahead of time, this will leave you with a little more time to spend with your companions.

When your guests arrive, offer a selection of tasty small bites, along with a glass of something chilled to get things going. If you really want to get the party started, serve some Champagne or sparkling wine and creative cocktails like Champagne Sidecar or Black Velvet are also great for sharing.

We include superb starters and magnificent main courses, followed by some truly decadent desserts. Appealing appetizers include first class classics like Asparagus with Hollandaise Sauce, Marinated Baked Ricotta with Roasted Vegetables or Roast Duck Salad.

For the main event, prove your proficiency in the kitchen and transfer taste buds to all corners of the globe. For meat enthusiasts, select from elaborate eats like Barbecued Asian Poussins or Pulled Pork with Sweet Potato Mash. Fish and seafood aficionados are sure to enjoy Seared Scallops with Fresh Mint & Red Chilli Dressing or Lobster Salad with Herbed Mayonnaise. For those who prefer to eat less meat and fish, Kale, Lemon & Chive Linguine or Wild Mushroom Risotto are fitting for a special meal.

Serve some sophisticated sides alongside the main star, like roast or hasselback potatoes, potatoes dauphinoise, rösti, vegetable gratins, creamed vegetables or creamy mash. Alternatively, simple sides such as steamed baby vegetables, tossed salads, stir-fried vegetables or roasted roots are ideal, especially if you are serving a rich and elaborate main course.

Make sure you save space for an indulgent sweet treat and choose from one of our sumptuous sensations. Stunning desserts include Roasted Fig Tartlets, Spiced Plum & Blackberry Brûlées or Mocha Soufflés with Mascarpone. For committed chocoholics, individual Hot Chocolate Desserts & Candied Oranges will certainly hit the spot.

On a slightly lighter note, Champagne Sorbet will provide an elegant and refreshing dessert, ideal for cleansing the palate after an indulgent meal, but if cheese is more your thing, check out Goat's Cheese with Honey & Walnuts.

Finally, it's well worth having some after-dinner coffee options on offer so that you can provide a welcome hot drink to pep things up after the big meal. Some people may prefer a digestif or nightcap, such as a glass of cognac, whisky or port, or a liquor-based cocktail, such as a White Russian or Brandy Alexander, to help their meal go down and to finish the night off in style.

# Creating the Perfect Dinner Party Menu

*When planning a menu for a special meal, the key word is balance. The meal needs to feel as though it flows from beginning to end. You do not want your guests to feel too full at the end of the meal but you do not want them to be hungry either so it's a hard balancing act. If you do serve a rich course, serve a lighter portion. If you feel the meal could be a little small then perhaps think about serving bread or rolls.*

Think about what food is going to be served before and after the main course. With good food, less is often more. Leave your guests pleased and satisfied. If you are going to have a creamy soup to start, you don't need to serve half a litre of the stuff to each person. Likewise, if you are serving your favourite rich chocolate cake for dessert, it can be a thin sliver rather than a great slab.

When deciding on what to cook, try not to have repetition of key ingredients, colours or textures throughout the meal. If, for example, you decide to serve walnut bread with a starter of soup, followed by lamb with an almond stuffing and then a hazelnut chocolate pudding, you have

an overwhelmingly nut-based menu. All the courses are delicious, but there is no balance to the meal and the flavours are samey. You have also created another problem: if any of the diners happens to suffer from a nut allergy, you will have to make an alternative dish for every course.

Another example of an unbalanced meal would be a cream of mushroom soup to start, followed by roast chicken and creamed mashed potato and a dessert of crème caramel. You have created three delicious dishes in varying shades of pale brown, white and cream, with little defining texture. Texture is vital to the creation of each dish as well as the overall balance of the meal.

Make sure that you don't serve only very soft food without any definition as it can just seem too mushy.

When setting out to prepare a special meal, do make sure you give yourself enough time to enjoy creating and preparing it. The main focuses should be the cooking and having a good time so try to get as much of the boring stuff done in advance so you can focus on being the chef and host for the evening. Do not try to leave work and then make an entire three-course dinner for guests who are arriving at 7.30 p.m. If you can shop the day before or during the day and maybe do a bit of the prep beforehand or make one of the dishes in advance it will really make all the difference.

Dishes such as soups, casseroles and curry pastes all lend themselves to being made in advance. Also some desserts can be made and then left to set in the refrigerator overnight. Then the dessert is guaranteed to be completely set and cold, which is one worry fewer for the evening, and you have managed to get at least one of the courses of the meal completely prepared in advance.

Before preparing the food, start by planning the order of preparation in an organized way that will work for you. In a kitchen, this is called time and motion. Get things baking in the oven or cooking slowly on the hob. Start any yeast-based bread and leave cold desserts to set before you do a job such as chopping herbs.

When you are chopping, washing up or setting the table, you are doing only one job at a time. However, if you have got three or four other jobs going on, then doing that one job will not be a waste of time or slow you down. This will leave you more time to make your food look beautiful and really well thought out on the plate, so it's worth fully planning the evening out and organizing your time well in advance.

Another time-saver is to set the table in the morning or even the night before. You may find this a little excessive and super-organized, but in a restaurant, the tables for lunch are always set up straight after dinner the evening before. This is because it saves a huge amount of time and makes the meal that much easier to prepare and serve, as all the focus is on the food. This will make the evening as a whole much more enjoyable and relaxing as at least you know that the table is ready. It also allows you to seat guests when they arrive so they are comfortable and enjoying a glass of wine while you finish off the last bits of preparation for the meal.

# Getting Ready for a Dinner Party

*It's Saturday evening and the guests are due any minute – you've got the wine perfectly chilled and the food is prepped and ready to go. It's time to put on some tunes and prepare for the fun and feasting ahead. Here is some advice on how to get the evening off to a great start and to keep the drinks, food and conversation flowing effortlessly.*

It is fine to have one course that requires some last-minute cooking, such as scallops for a main course. However, if every course has lots of last-minute cooking, you will spend the whole evening in the kitchen, missing out on all the banter and apologizing to your guests for not being at the table with them.

Remember that herbs and salad leaves should be prepped at the last minute, so that they do not spoil. Prep all similar ingredients at the same time. If garlic will be used in more than one course, chop it as one batch, then use it as needed.

When choosing the cutlery and crockery that you are going to use for each course, count them out into a pile. If you are cooking for four people, you should have enough matching plates, but if you are cooking for 12 or more, the quantities are going to be harder to keep tabs on.

It's fine to have to quickly wash the starter plate to be re-used for dessert, because you should have time to do it, but if you don't have enough, try to borrow some crockery and cutlery from friends so you don't have to spend too long in the kitchen between courses. Also, you don't want your guests to be waiting a long time for their main course or dessert.

The type of crockery and the other table dressings are very important for setting the right mood. Using candles or tealights can transform a simple dinner into something more stylish and sumptuous. Flowers on the table add colour, although you should avoid strongly scented flowers, such as lilies, as they can overpower the aromas of the food.

Only use multicoloured or patterned plates to serve something that has very few colours. The rich red of a tomato soup could work in a blue patterned bowl. If your food has a lot of colours, shades and shapes, it will sit much better on a plain white dish. The most elegant table settings are the most simple. Too many flavours on a plate do not make better food, and the same is true of presentation – too many contrasts of colour and shape will over-complicate things and you will lose your focus.

Think about the colours and shapes and how they will best contrast and complement the plates and tableware. Some dishes, such as modern Asian food, may work on a square or rectangular plate, but not everything does. A dish from Spain, the Middle East or Morocco will look good in a simple, glazed terracotta dish. More contemporary dishes will be better on large, flat white plates; other dishes will look better when served in slightly shallow, light-coloured dishes.

1    2    3

# Asparagus with Hollandaise Sauce

*This classic dish makes a simple but impressive starter. Once you have mastered making your own smooth and creamy hollandaise sauce, it is also good for accompanying poached fish or grilled chicken, fish or steaks.*

**SERVES 4**
Prepares in 20–25 minutes,
 plus cooling
Cooks in 15 minutes

650 g/1 lb 7 oz asparagus, trimmed

### Hollandaise Sauce
4 tbsp white wine vinegar
½ tbsp finely chopped shallots
5 black peppercorns
1 bay leaf
3 large egg yolks
140 g/5 oz unsalted butter, finely diced
2 tsp lemon juice
salt
pinch of cayenne pepper

1. Divide the asparagus into four bundles and tie each with kitchen string, criss-crossing the string from just below the tips to the base. Stand the bundles upright in a deep saucepan. Add boiling water to come three quarters of the way up the stalks, then cover with a loose tent of foil, shiny-side down, inside the pan. Heat the water until bubbles appear around the side of the pan, then simmer for 10 minutes, or until the stalks are just tender when pierced with the tip of a knife. Drain well and remove the string.

2. Meanwhile, to make the hollandaise sauce, boil the vinegar, shallots, peppercorns and bay leaf in a saucepan over a high heat until reduced to 1 tablespoon. Cool slightly, then strain into a heatproof bowl that will fit over a saucepan of simmering water.

3. Beat the egg yolks into the bowl. Set the bowl over the pan of simmering water and whisk the egg yolks constantly until they are thick enough to leave a trail on the surface.

4. Take care to not let the water boil. Gradually beat in the butter, piece by piece, whisking constantly until the sauce is like soft mayonnaise. Stir in the lemon juice, then add salt to taste and the cayenne pepper. Serve the sauce immediately with the asparagus.

# Baked Seafood with Fresh Coriander Chutney

These parcels make a great start
to a meal as everyone receives
their own package and then
gets to experience opening
it. There is great contrast
between the bright green
sauce and the pink prawns.

12 large raw prawns, peeled
   and deveined
1 kg/2 lb 4 oz live mussels, scrubbed
   and debearded
8 scallops
400 g/14 oz firm white fish, such as sea
   bream or snapper, skinned and cubed

2.5-cm/1-inch piece of fresh ginger,
   chopped
½ tsp salt
1 green chilli, deseeded and
   finely chopped
25 g/1 oz fresh coriander
100 ml/3½ fl oz coconut cream

1. For the chutney, cover the desiccated coconut with boiling water and leave to stand for 40 minutes. Roast the coriander seeds in a dry frying pan over a medium heat for 2 minutes until fragrant. Take care not to scorch them.

2. Crush the roasted coriander seeds. Place in a food processor with the garlic, ginger and salt and work into a rough paste. Add the chilli and blend until smooth. Strain the coconut, reserving the soaking liquid. Add the coconut to the blender with two thirds of the fresh coriander.

3. Continue to blend this mixture until smooth and bright green. Add some of the coconut soaking liquid to help combine the mixture. Remove the mixture and place in a bowl. Stir in the coconut cream and lime juice. Taste and adjust the seasoning. This chutney is best used fresh but it will keep, covered, in the refrigerator for a couple of days.

4. You could use any combination of seafood, such as prawns, crayfish, lobster, crab, squid, mussels and fish. Make sure the fish is cleaned, boned and scaled and the shellfish is cleaned. Wash the shellfish until the water runs completely clear. Remove any shellfish that does not close when you tap them and remove any that smell.

5. To make the parcels, fold a large rectangle of baking paper in half, so the two shorter ends meet. Fold in half again, so that the two shorter ends meet. Hold by the two shorter ends and fold each end over slightly, by about 2.5 cm/ 1 inch. You should have an envelope that is open at one end with two folded edges at the sides. Repeat with three other baking paper rectangles. Rub a little oil on the inside of the envelopes. Season the seafood with a little salt and pepper.

6. Preheat the oven to 200°C/400°F/Gas Mark 6 and preheat two baking sheets. Mix the chutney with the seafood and then divide the mixture between the envelopes. Fold the open end of each envelope tightly to seal. These envelopes could be made, filled and kept in the refrigerator for a couple of hours before you need them. Place the filled envelopes flat on the preheated baking sheets and bake in the preheated oven for 10 minutes.

7. When ready to serve, transfer the parcels to plates and allow your guests to open them so that they get all the aromas. Warn them to be careful with the steam because it may come out in a jet. Any shellfish that still has not opened should be discarded. Garnish the parcels with the remaining fresh coriander.

# Marinated Baked Ricotta with Roasted Vegetables

Marinated fresh ricotta cheese and roasted mixed vegetables combine beautifully with a zingy lemon-herb dressing to create this mouth-watering meat-free salad, excellent served as a sensational starter before a meaty main course.

**SERVES 6**
Prepares in 50 minutes,
 plus cooling
Cooks in 35 minutes

2 whole ricotta cheeses, 200 g/7 oz each
2 sweet potatoes, cut into
 3-cm/1¼-inch cubes
1 butternut squash, cut into
 3-cm/1¼-inch cubes
2 fennel bulbs
100 g/3½ oz pine nuts
2 handfuls mixed bitter
 and peppery salad leaves
olive oil
salt and pepper

### Marinade
½ red chilli
3 tbsp olive oil
juice of 1 lemon

### Dressing
½ garlic clove, finely chopped
pinch of salt
small bunch of fresh basil,
 roughly chopped, plus extra leaves
juice and zest of 1 lemon
4 tbsp extra virgin olive oil

1. Preheat the oven to 200°C/400°F/ Gas Mark 6. For the marinade, deseed and finely chop the chilli, then mix with the olive oil and lemon juice.

2. Add the whole ricotta cheeses to the marinade. Turn the cheeses regularly in the marinade. Brush the cubes of sweet potato and butternut squash with a little oil and season with salt and pepper. Place in a roasting tin and roast in the oven for about 20 minutes, until caramelized and golden.

3. Halve the fennel bulbs, removing the tough outside layer, then carefully chop each half into thin wedges.

4. Dry-roast the pine nuts on a separate baking tray in the preheated oven and roast until golden brown in colour.

5. For the dressing, crush the garlic with the salt to a fine purée. Place the garlic and most of the chopped basil in a food processor and pulse to a paste. Add the lemon juice and zest and work until smooth, and then stir in the olive oil (or you can use some of the oil from the marinade). Check the seasoning and add more salt and pepper to taste.

6. Heat an ovenproof frying pan over a medium–high heat. Add the whole ricotta cheeses and brown on one side for 2–3 minutes. Gently turn over – if it's too fragile to turn, just brown on one side. Scatter the fennel around the pan, season well with salt and pepper and transfer to the oven for 5 minutes.

7. When the sweet potato and butternut squash are cooked (they should be soft to the point of a knife) leave to cool slightly, then place in a bowl and dress with two thirds of the basil dressing. Add the salad leaves, tearing any that are too big. Tear in the extra basil leaves. If you break the herbs into the salad just before serving you will get the aromas and perfumes of the herbs. Add the fennel and then gently break in the ricotta cheese. Mix together lightly to avoid it turning mushy.

8. Place an 8-cm/3½-inch round biscuit cutter or ring on each plate and gently fill with the roasted vegetables and mixed salad. Pour the remaining dressing over the salad and garnish with the remaining chopped basil and roasted pine nuts. Remove the cutters and serve immediately.

# Roast Duck Salad with Orange & Warm Hazelnut Vinaigrette

*Succulent roasted duck breasts and juicy fresh orange segments create the perfect pairing, while roasted hazelnuts, watercress and mint leaves add extra crunch and flavour to this tantalizing warm salad starter.*

SERVES 4–6
Prepares in 35–40 minutes
Cooks in 30 minutres

2–3 duck breasts
100 g/3½ oz hazelnuts
200 g/7 oz watercress
4 oranges, peeled, segmented
   and pith removed
30 fresh mint leaves, plus extra to garnish
4 shallots, halved, cored and
   very finely sliced
salt and pepper

## Vinaigrette

50 ml/2 fl oz orange juice
1 tbsp fresh thyme leaves
50 ml/2 fl oz extra virgin olive oil
2 tbsp red wine vinegar
2 tbsp hazelnut oil or walnut oil
salt and pepper

1. Preheat the oven to 200°C/400°F/Gas Mark 6. Trim the excess fat off of the duck breasts and season to taste with salt and pepper.

2. Place the duck breasts skin-side down in a frying pan over a low heat. Cook for about 15 minutes, or until the skin is crisp and the fat is gone. Strain off any excess fat while you are cooking.

3. Roast the hazelnuts on a baking tray in the preheated oven for about 5 minutes, or until the nuts have turned a golden brown.

4. Place the roasted nuts in a clean tea towel and rub vigorously to remove the skins. Place in a food processor and pulse until the nuts are roughly chopped.

5. Season the duck breasts again with salt and pepper to taste and place them flesh-side down in a roasting tin. Roast the duck in the preheated oven for 8 minutes, or until completely cooked through. Check that the centre of the meat is no longer pink and that the juices run clear when the thickest part of the meat is skewered with a knife – they should be cooked to medium.

6. Remove the duck breasts from the oven and leave to rest.

7. Put the vinaigrette ingredients into a small saucepan and place over a low heat until warm. Do not allow to boil. When ready to serve, place the watercress in the bowl with the orange segments. Tear the mint and add the sliced shallots.

8. Thinly slice the warm duck breasts. Add to the bowl. Add any juices from the duck breasts to the vinaigrette.

9. Add half of the chopped hazelnuts to the vinaigrette.

10. Serve the salad on individual plates, building up layers of oranges, salad leaves, slices of duck and most of the remaining hazelnuts. Spoon the warm dressing over the top and then garnish each dish with any remaining chopped nuts and some torn mint.

# Top Ten Styling Tips

*A meal that is well presented with a visual flair can make all the difference to your enjoyment of the food. Learn how to serve your food with style, with the help of these top tips which are simple but can add real appeal to your dishes.*

1. Think of the plate or dish that you are serving on as though it were a picture frame – and remember that it has to suit the picture you have painted.

2. Plate regional food that is from particular countries or particular areas on plates, dishes and platters that come from those regions, or have the same look.

3. Too many colours and patterns on crockery or table accessories will take the focus off the food. It's better to keep it simple rather than overcomplicating the colour scheme.

4. Keep your food styling simple and elegant so that you allow nature's produce, and your hard work, to speak for themselves.

5. Candles and tealights can soften the mood and make a table look more elegant. If you have to use electric lights, see if they can be dimmed or use small lamps that are less harsh. Coloured glass Moroccan-style tealight holders or Asian paper lanterns can also create a great atmosphere for eating.

6. For the most effective results, carry a simple colour scheme through the table accessories, such as the napkins and flowers. For example, you could have a white tablecloth, blue and white napkins and blue and white flowers on the table to add a really simple splash of colour to a setting.

7. Take care to clean away any fingerprints and splashes of gravy or sauce from the edges of the plates for a really professional finish. In restaurants, they use a clean cloth dipped in a mixture of water and a little vinegar. The acid cleans away grease rather than just spreading any oil around the edges of the plates.

8. When plating food, place it in the centre of the plate and build up the layers of texture to create some central height on the plate. You don't want your food to look like the leaning tower of Pisa, so aim for layers that are rising elegantly to a central point.

9. When plating dishes for a lot of people at a buffet or a barbecue, use flat dishes and platters rather than bowls. It is always going to be more visually appealing to look up at something, than to look down at something in the bottom of a bowl.

10. When arranging a number of larger dishes on a buffet table, vary the eye line to draw attention to the different types of food. Place some upside-down bowls or books under the tablecloth to create raised plinths for highlighting certain dishes that you think are extra special.

# Top Ten Garnishing Tips

*Garnishing can add real colour and style to your finished dishes. Just a simple dash of chopped herbs can dress up a dish that was in danger of looking drearily brown. Style up your food with these top garnishing tips.*

1. Allow simple contrasting colours to draw the eye to the food – for example, simple combinations such as red and white or orange and white can be very effective and eye-catching.

2. Use texture to your advantage to create irregular textural differences that are visually exciting. The reason canned fruit salad looks so unappealing is because the contents are all uniform in size. When making a salad, cut each fruit or vegetable in a different way so that the eye will be drawn to the variations in shape and size.

3. Present things in uneven numbers, for example three or five scallops. When things are presented in uneven numbers, your eye is interested and your brain is stimulated by the imperfection.

4. Allow the ingredients in the dish to form part of the garnish, for example chopped roasted nuts or pomegranate seeds, or torn mint or coriander leaves. This creates a consistency of flavours, as well as adding visual appeal.

5. Use brightly coloured ingredients, such as beetroot, pumpkin and sweet potato, and coloured spices, such as saffron and turmeric, to add a naturally coloured garnish to dishes.

6. Use fresh herbs to make some flavoured, coloured oils and dressings, such as basil or coriander oil. These can be drizzled attractively over dishes to add some colour and style.

7. To make the dressing of a plate straightforward and professional-looking, buy some small, clear squeezy bottles. Any sauces or dressings can be poured into the bottle and applied neatly to the plate with a flick of the wrist.

8. Allow the naturally beautiful form of an ingredient to be appreciated for its own merits when serving foods such as cooked mushrooms, slices of fennel, halved figs and asparagus spears. These are shaped in a visually appealing way so look great just as they are.

9. Keep the number of components in a dish to a minimum, so that each piece has a relevance and adds an appropriate balance to the overall dish. Overcrowded dishes can look automatically less stylish.

10. Ingredients such as honey, caramel or oil can make the elements of the most plain dish look bright and vibrant and sumptuous. Think of how beautiful natural yogurt simply drizzled with honey can be. Dress the dish with the sauce or dressing just before you serve it to ensure this effect.

# Rib-eye Steak, Chimichurri Sauce & Mash

*Piquant chimichurri sauce complements the griddled rib-eye steaks perfectly in this tempting main course for two. Accompanied by creamy sweet potato mash, this is a great date-night meal.*

**SERVES 2**
Prepares in 30 minutes
Cooks in 25–30 minutes,
  plus resting

1 tbsp olive oil
2 x 125 g/4½ oz rib-eye steaks
½ tsp ground cumin
salt and pepper

## Chimichurri Sauce
15 g/½ oz fresh flat-leaf parsley,
  roughly chopped
15 g/½ oz fresh oregano
3 small garlic cloves, roughly chopped
½ shallot, roughly chopped
¼ red chilli, deseeded
  and roughly chopped

3 tbsp extra virgin olive oil
1 tsp red wine vinegar
juice of ¼ lemon

## Mash
250 g/9 oz sweet potatoes,
  cut into 2-cm/¾-inch chunks
20 g/¾ butter

1. To make the mash, cook the sweet potatoes in a large saucepan of lightly salted boiling water for 12–15 minutes, or until very soft. Drain, then leave off the heat to steam dry in the pan for at least 5 minutes. Using a potato masher, mash the potatoes to a smooth consistency.

2. Meanwhile, to make the chimichurri sauce, put all the ingredients in a food processor, season with salt and pepper, and process until you have a paste of a similar consistency to pesto. Add a little extra olive oil if the mixture appears too thick. Spoon into a serving bowl, cover and set aside.

3. Return the mash to the heat and warm through before stirring in the butter. Season with salt and pepper, and keep warm.

4. Massage the oil into both sides of each steak, then sprinkle with salt and the cumin. Heat a griddle pan over a high heat until smoking hot. Cook each steak for 2–3 minutes on each side, or for longer if you prefer it well done. Allow the steaks to rest for 2 minutes.

5. Serve a steak on each of two plates with the chimichurri sauce spooned over and the mash on the side.

# Slow-cooked Lamb Shanks with Gremolata

*These really flavourful slow-cooked lamb shanks are given a tantalizing twist with a scattering of roasted almond gremolata just before serving.*

**SERVES 4**
Prepares in 25–30 minutes
Cooks in 2 hours 55 minutes

4 trimmed lamb shanks
2 tbsp olive oil
4 garlic cloves, halved
1 dried chilli, crushed
3 rosemary sprigs
6 ripe plum tomatoes
2 large onions, finely chopped
4 strips orange zest
2 bay leaves
1 tsp brown sugar
100 ml/3½ fl oz red wine
500 ml/18 fl oz water
salt and pepper

### Gremolata
100 g/3½ oz blanched skinless almonds
2 garlic cloves, finely chopped
zest of 2 lemons
small bunch of fresh flat-leaf parsley, chopped

1. Preheat the oven to 180°C/350°F/Gas Mark 4. Season the lamb shanks well with salt and pepper. Heat 1 tablespoon of the oil in a large, heavy-based flameproof casserole. Add the meat to the casserole dish and brown on all sides for 3 minutes, then remove from the heat. Chop the garlic, chilli and rosemary together.

2. Cut the tomatoes in half and, with the skin side in your hand, grate the flesh on a cheese grater to form a rough tomato pulp. The skin will be left in your hand.

3. Remove the meat from the casserole dish and return the casserole to the heat with 1 tablespoon of the oil. Add the garlic, chilli and rosemary and fry briskly for 2 minutes, or until fragrant and aromatic. Add the onions to the casserole and cook for about 5 minutes, or until soft. Season to taste with with salt and pepper.

4. Return the meat to the casserole dish with the orange zest, bay leaves, sugar, tomato pulp, wine and water. Stir until everything is thoroughly combined.

5. Cover and bring the mixture to a simmer over a medium–high heat on the hob. Transfer the casserole to the preheated oven and cook for a further 2½ hours, basting regularly. Check the seasoning again and add more salt and pepper, if desired.

6. Meanwhile, to make the gremolata, roast the almonds in the preheated oven for 3 minutes, or until golden brown.

7. Make sure the garlic is very finely chopped as this is being eaten raw. Place the chopped garlic into a small bowl. Add the cooled almonds and the lemon zest to the bowl and mix to thoroughly combine.

8. When ready to serve, mix the parsley into the gremolata. Scatter the gremolata over the cooked lamb shanks and serve immediately.

# Barbecued Asian Poussins

*Ideal for al fresco summertime eating, prepare these marinated poussins in advance, then simply barbecue them when you are ready to eat. Served with a tangy salad, this fantastic flavourful dish will thrill your guests.*

SERVES 4
Prepares in 35–40 minutes,
  plus marinating
Cooks in 40–50 minutes,
  plus resting

2 poussins, about 450 g/1 lb each,
  spatchcocked
1 orange, thinly sliced
4 tbsp extra virgin olive oil,
  plus extra for oiling
1½ tbsp fresh orange juice
1 tsp sesame oil
400 g/14 oz fresh watercress leaves,
  trimmed, rinsed and thoroughly dried
1 red pepper, thinly shredded with a
  vegetable peeler
2 tbsp sesame seeds, toasted
salt and pepper
chopped fresh coriander, to garnish

## Marinade
6 tbsp sunflower oil
4 tbsp soy sauce
2 tbsp sesame oil
2 garlic cloves, very finely chopped
1-cm/½-inch piece fresh ginger, grated
pinch chilli flakes, to taste

1. To make the marinade, mix all the ingredients together in a non-metallic bowl large enough to hold both poussins, then set aside.

2. Ease the skin from the breast flesh on both birds. Gently slide the orange slices under the skin, then ease the skin back over the slices. Put the poussins in the marinade and rub the mixture all over. Cover with clingfilm and leave to marinate in the refrigerator for 4–24 hours, turning occasionally.

3. Remove the poussins from the refrigerator 20 minutes in advance of cooking.

4. Preheat the barbecue. Brush the barbecue rack with olive oil and position it about 10 cm/ 4 inches above the heat. Spear each poussin with two long metal skewers, from left to right at the top and bottom, to keep them flat.

5. Put the birds on the grill rack, breast-side down, and grill for 20–25 minutes on each side, basting occasionally with the remaining marinade. Grill until the birds are cooked through and until the juices run clear when the thickest part of the thighs are pierced and there is no pink meat.

6. Leave to rest for 10 minutes, then cut each bird in half and remove the orange slices.

7. Alternatively, preheat the oven to 180°C/350°F/Gas Mark 4. Heat a large ridged cast-iron griddle pan over a high heat until a splash of water 'dances' on the surface. Brush with olive oil, then add the unskewered birds and griddle for 10 minutes, or until browned.

8. Turn the birds over and put the pan in the preheated oven for a further 30 minutes, basting occasionally with the remaining marinade, until the juices run clear when the thickest parts of the thighs are pierced and there is no pink meat.

9. Meanwhile, mix the olive oil, orange juice and sesame oil with salt and pepper to taste in a non-metallic bowl. Add the watercress, pepper and sesame seeds and toss together.

10. Arrange a portion of salad on each plate and serve with half a poussin on top. Sprinkle with coriander and serve hot or at room temperature.

# Hearty Beef Stew with Herby Cheese Dumplings & Kale

*A warming, comforting dish using seasonal ingredients that is perfect for a cold winter evening. Get the fire roaring, break out a bottle of full-bodied red wine and this stew is sure to hit the spot with any hungry guests.*

**SERVES 4**
Prepares in 40 minutes
Cooks in 2 hours 55 minutes–
 3 hours 25 minutes

4 tbsp olive oil
½ onion, finely chopped
1 leek, thinly sliced
1 celery stick, roughly chopped
4 garlic cloves, finely chopped
1 tsp tomato purée
900 g/2 lb beef shin, cut into
 bite-sized chunks
40 g/1½ oz quinoa flour
125 ml/4 fl oz brandy
800 ml/1 pint 7 fl oz beef stock
1 tbsp fresh thyme leaves
2 tbsp finely chopped fresh
 flat-leaf parsley
2 tsp smoked paprika
6 cloves

2 bay leaves
salt and pepper
200 g/7 oz kale, roughly chopped, to serve
juice of ¼ lemon, to serve

## Dumplings
125 g/4½ oz quinoa flour
20 g/¾ oz beef suet
60 g/2¼ oz mature Cheddar cheese,
 grated
1 tsp baking powder
1 tbsp fresh thyme leaves
2 tbsp finely chopped fresh
 flat-leaf parsley
4 tbsp water

1. Heat 2 tablespoons of the oil in a large lidded casserole over a medium heat. Add the onion, leek and celery, and fry for 5 minutes, or until softened.

2. Add the garlic and tomato purée, stir well, then turn the heat down to medium–low and leave to simmer while you cook the meat.

3. Heat the remaining 2 tablespoons of the oil in a large, heavy-based frying pan over a high heat until smoking hot. Season the beef with salt and pepper, then add it to the pan in batches and cook for a few minutes, turning, until browned on all sides.

4. Using a slotted spoon, transfer the first batch to a plate while you brown the rest of the meat. Toss the browned meat into the casserole, then stir in the quinoa flour.

5. Turn the heat down to medium–high. Deglaze the beef frying pan with the brandy, being careful as it can flame. Scrape all the meaty goodness off the bottom of the pan into the bubbling brandy with a wooden spoon, then tip into the casserole. Pour in the stock, then add the thyme, parsley, paprika, cloves and bay leaves, and season with salt and pepper.

6. Bring to a boil, then turn the heat down to low and cover. Simmer for 2–2½ hours, or until the sauce is thick and the meat is soft enough to pull apart with a spoon.

7. To make the dumplings, put the quinoa flour, suet, cheese, baking powder, thyme and parsley in a large bowl and mix well. Add the water a little at a time, mixing, until you have a firm dough. Shape the mixture into 12 small balls.

8. After 2–2½ hours cooking, remove the lid from the stew and arrange the dumplings on top. Put the lid back on and cook for 20 minutes, or until the dumplings are cooked through.

9. Cook the kale in a large pan of lightly salted boiling water for 2 minutes. Drain, then squeeze over the lemon juice and toss lightly. Serve immediately with the stew.

# Barbecue Pulled Pork with Sweet Potato Mash

*Slow-cooked barbecued pork produces really tender, juicy shreds of tasty meat, which is then tossed in home-made chilli sauce and served with sweet potato mash. Perfect for outdoor summer eating with family or a group of friends.*

SERVES 6–8
Prepares in 35–40 minutes
Cooks in 12 hours 20 minutes,
  plus resting

3 kg/6 lb 8 oz pork shoulder,
  skin removed and bone in

### Rub

1 tbsp paprika
2 tbsp light brown sugar
1 tsp dried thyme
1 tsp dried oregano
2 tsp pepper
1 tsp garlic salt
1 tsp celery salt
1 tsp salt
1 tsp onion powder

### Chilli Sauce

2 tbsp yellow American-style mustard
2 tbsp cider vinegar
2 tbsp treacle
2 tbsp tomato ketchup
1 tbsp sriracha chilli sauce

### Sweet Potato Mash

1 kg/2 lb 4 oz sweet potatoes, diced
200 g/7 oz salted butter, diced
1 tsp pepper

1. Preheat the barbecue to a very low heat.

2. Combine all of the rub ingredients together in a small bowl.

3. Place the pork on a chopping board and massage the rub all over the pork.

4. Place the pork on the barbecue grill, making sure the pork is fat-side up. Close the lid and cook for 12 hours, or until a thick, dark golden crust has formed. Check that the centre of the meat is no longer pink and that the juices run clear. Cover in foil and leave to rest in a warm place for 30 minutes.

5. To make the sauce, mix together all of the ingredients in a small bowl. Set aside.

6. Boil or steam the sweet potatoes in a large saucepan until soft when pricked with a knife. Drain and mash, then beat in the butter and pepper.

7. Remove any bones from the pork and pull the meat into large chunks. The meat should be very tender, so this should not be hard to do. Put the pork in a large bowl and tip over the chilli sauce. Gently mix, trying not to break up the pork too much.

8. Serve the pork with the sweet potato mash.

# Kale, Lemon & Chive Linguine

*This tempting meat-free dish boasts a simple but fantastic fusion of fresh flavours, with the vibrant green of kale and chives adding to its appeal. Serve with a simple leaf salad and warm fresh crusty bread.*

**SERVES 2–3**
Prepares in 15–20 minutes
Cooks in 20 minutes

250 g/9 oz kale, thick stems removed,
   leaves sliced crossways
   into thin ribbons
225 g/8 oz dried linguine
8 tbsp olive oil
1 onion, chopped
1 garlic clove, very thinly sliced
grated rind of 1 large lemon
large pinch of dried red chilli flakes
3 tbsp snipped fresh chives
4 tbsp freshly grated Parmesan cheese
salt and pepper

1. Bring a large saucepan of water to the boil. Add the kale and blanch for 2 minutes, or until just wilted. Drain the kale, reserving the water, and set aside.

2. Return the reserved water to the saucepan and bring to the boil. Add the linguine and cook for 10–12 minutes, or until tender but still firm to the bite.

3. Meanwhile, heat the oil in a large frying pan over a medium–high heat. Add the onion and fry for 2–3 minutes, or until translucent. Add the garlic and fry for a further minute.

4. Stir in the kale, lemon rind and chilli flakes and season to taste with salt and pepper. Cook over a medium heat for 4–5 minutes, stirring occasionally, until tender but still bright green. Add a little of the cooking water if the mixture becomes dry.

5. Drain the pasta and tip into a warmed serving dish. Add the kale mixture, tossing with the pasta to mix. Stir in the chives and Parmesan with salt and pepper to taste. Toss again and serve immediately.

# Seared Scallops with Fresh Mint & Red Chilli Dressing

Prove your cooking prowess with this wonderful combination of seared fresh scallops served on a bed of peppery salad leaves, with herby Puy lentils, crisp pan-fried pancetta and a drizzle of mint-chilli dressing.

SERVES 4–6
Prepares in 35 minutes
Cooks in 25–28 minutes

100 g/3½ oz Puy lentils
2 garlic cloves
1 celery stick
2 bay leaves
20 fresh parsley leaves, with stalks
olive oil, for drizzling and frying
juice and zest of 1 lemon
2 tbsp aged red wine vinegar
20 fresh basil leaves, roughly chopped
20 fresh mint leaves, roughly chopped
handful of rocket leaves, roughly chopped
20 scallops
8 slices pancetta
salt and pepper
peppery salad leaves, to serve

## Mint & Red Chilli Dressing
2 red chillies, deseeded and chopped
small bunch of fresh mint, finely chopped
100 ml/3½ fl oz extra virgin olive oil
juice of 1 lemon
salt and pepper

1. Cover the lentils with cold water in a large saucepan and add the garlic, celery stick and bay leaves. Add a few parsley stalks, bring to the boil, then reduce to a simmer.

2. Cook the lentil mixture for 12–15 minutes, until they are al dente and nutty. Taste them periodically so that they are not overcooked and soggy. Remove from the heat and drain off most of the water. Remove the garlic, bay leaves, celery stick and parsley stalks. Season the lentils with olive oil, lemon juice and zest, some of the vinegar, and salt and pepper. Seasoning them when they are hot will help the lentils absorb all the flavours.

3. When the lentils have cooled slightly, add the mixed chopped herbs and rocket and stir until thoroughly combined. Set the lentils aside until ready to serve.

4. For the dressing, mix together the chillies and mint in a bowl with the olive oil and the lemon juice, and season with salt and pepper.

5. Clean the scallops by removing the small opaque muscle from the sides, then dry the scallops on kitchen paper. Add a tablespoon of oil to a frying pan over a high heat, add the slices of pancetta and fry them for about 2 minutes on each side, until crispy. Drain on kitchen paper.

6. Keep the frying pan over a high heat. Pat the scallops until they are dry and then season them with salt and pepper to taste. Add a splash more olive oil to the frying pan.

7. Add the scallops and cook for 45 seconds. To turn the scallops, quickly use two tablespoons, one in each hand. Flick the scallops over from one spoon to the other.

8. Cook on the second side for about 40 seconds; when the scallops are caramelized on both sides remove and place on clean kitchen paper.

9. Add a splash of vinegar to deglaze the frying pan, then add the liquid to the dressing.

10. To serve, arrange some peppery salad leaves on each plate and scatter the warm herb lentils over the top. Arrange some scallops on each plate and place the crisp pancetta on top. Spoon over some of the mint and chilli dressing and serve immediately.

# Wild Mushroom Risotto

*Take your time to cook this classic recipe and your patience will be rewarded with an exquisitely creamy and flavourful mushroom risotto, perfect for a meat-free meal for sharing with friends at the weekend.*

**SERVES 6**
Prepares in 20 minutes,
  plus soaking
Cooks in 30–40 minutes

55 g/2 oz dried porcini mushrooms
about 500 g/1 lb 2 oz mixed fresh
  wild mushrooms, such as field
  mushrooms and chanterelles,
  halved if large
4 tbsp olive oil
3–4 garlic cloves, finely chopped
55 g/2 oz butter
1 onion, finely chopped
350 g/12 oz risotto rice

50 ml/2 fl oz dry white vermouth
1.2 litres/2 pints vegetable stock
115 g/4 oz freshly grated Parmesan
  cheese
4 tbsp chopped fresh flat-leaf parsley
salt and pepper

1. Place the dried mushrooms in a heatproof bowl and add boiling water to cover. Set aside to soak for 30 minutes, then carefully lift out and pat dry. Strain the soaking liquid through a sieve lined with kitchen paper and set aside.

2. Trim the fresh mushrooms. Heat 3 tablespoons of the oil in a large frying pan. Add the fresh mushrooms and stir-fry for 1–2 minutes. Add the garlic and the soaked mushrooms and cook, stirring frequently, for 2 minutes. Transfer to a plate.

3. Heat the remaining oil and half of the butter in a large, heavy-based saucepan. Add the onion and cook over a medium heat, stirring occasionally, for 2 minutes, or until softened.

4. Reduce the heat, stir in the rice and cook, stirring constantly, for 2–3 minutes, or until the grains are translucent. Add the vermouth and cook for 1 minute until reduced.

5. Gradually add the hot stock, a ladleful at a time, until all the liquid is absorbed. Add half of the reserved mushroom soaking liquid to the risotto and stir in the mushrooms. Season to taste and add more mushroom liquid, if necessary. Stir in the remaining butter, grated Parmesan and chopped parsley and serve.

# Lobster Salad with Herbed Mayonnaise à la Parisienne

*Flaunt your flair with this really impressive fresh lobster salad accompanied by home-made herby mayonnaise. Serve with potatoes and lettuce leaves and you'll have created the ultimate salad of the season!*

**SERVES 4**
Prepares in 40 minutes, plus
  freezing, cooling and chilling
Cooks in 20 minutes

2 live lobsters, around 750 g/1 lb 12 oz,
  or 500 g/1 lb 2 oz cooked fresh
  lobster meat
1 large cucumber
1 lettuce
4 hard-boiled eggs, halved
salt and pepper
steamed or boiled new potatoes
  and lettuce leaves, to serve

### Mayonnaise
2 egg yolks
1 tsp Dijon mustard
100 ml/3½ fl oz extra virgin olive oil
150 ml/5 fl oz sunflower oil
1 tbsp lemon juice
4 tbsp cold water
small handful of fresh parsley,
  finely chopped
small handful of fresh dill, finely chopped
small handful of fresh chervil (optional),
  finely chopped
salt and pepper

1. If using fresh lobsters, put them into the freezer for 2 hours to kill them. Bring a large saucepan of heavily salted water to a boil and add the lobsters. Return to a boil and cook for 15 minutes. Remove from the heat, drain and let cool.

2. To make the mayonnaise, combine the egg yolks and mustard in a food processor. Turn the processor on and, with the motor running, pour in the olive oil and then the sunflower oil in a slow, regular trickle, until the mixture has a good thick consistency. Add the lemon juice, water, and salt and pepper to taste and pulse again. Fold the herbs through, then place in a bowl and refrigerate until ready to use.

3. Peel, halve, and seed the cucumber. Cut into thin slivers using a vegetable peeler.

4. Cut the lobster in half lengthwise, remove the dark vein that runs along the back of the tail, then remove the stomach sac that sits behind the mouth. Crack the claws with the back of a heavy knife.

5. Lay a bed of lettuce on each plate, scatter some cucumber over, then lay the egg halves and the halved lobsters on top. Season with salt and pepper, add the herby mayonnaise and serve with potatoes and more lettuce leaves.

# Parsi-style Baked Fish Wrapped in Banana Leaves

*Wow your gathered guests with this simple but very striking fish dish. Serve each diner their own sealed banana leaf parcel and enjoy their delight as they unwrap and discover a succulent, spicy fish fillet inside.*

SERVES 4
Prepares in 25–30 minutes
Cooks in 15–20 minutes

4 thick cod fillets, about 200 g/7 oz each, skinned
2 tsp ground turmeric
1 large fresh banana leaf

### Spice Paste

2 tsp ground cumin
2 tsp ground coriander
1½ tsp palm sugar
200 ml/7 fl oz coconut cream
4 red chillies, deseeded and chopped
100 g/3½ oz chopped fresh coriander
4 tbsp chopped fresh mint
5 garlic cloves, chopped
1 tsp finely grated fresh ginger
4 tbsp vegetable or groundnut oil
juice of 2 limes
2 tsp salt

1. Preheat the oven to 200°C/400°F/Gas Mark 6.

2. Place the fish fillets in a single layer on a plate and sprinkle over the turmeric. Rub into the fish and set aside.

3. Place the ingredients for the spice paste in a food processor and blend until fairly smooth. Set aside.

4. Cut the banana leaf into four 24-cm/9½-inch squares. Soften the banana leaf squares by dipping them into a pan of very hot water for a few seconds. Once they have become pliant, wipe them dry with kitchen paper and arrange on a work surface.

5. Apply the spice paste liberally to both sides of each piece of fish. Place a piece of fish on top of each banana leaf square and wrap up like a parcel, securing with bamboo skewers or string.

6. Place the parcels on a baking tray and bake in the preheated oven for 15–20 minutes, or until cooked through. Transfer to plates and serve immediately.

# Winning Wine Tips

*Whether you are a wine connoisseur or a relative novice, when it comes to matching wine with food there are no set rules as it's often down to a matter of personal taste. However, some specific wines do pair well with certain foods, while other more versatile wines match with a wider variety of foods.*

Many supermarkets, wine merchants, wine producers and online warehouses offer expert advice, including recommendations on which wines are good partners for different foods. Wine labels (shelf and bottle labels) often include useful tips on this too, or you may have your own long-standing favourites that will suit your meal perfectly.

Generally speaking, the most dominant ingredient or flavour in the dish you are serving is the one you want to match the wine with. You're aiming for a balance so that the wine and food complement each other and neither one overpowers the other.

For example, more delicate or light-flavoured foods like simple chicken, white fish, pasta or rice dishes are often best when partnered with soft, lighter wines (primarily white wines, but some light red wines too), whereas stronger, heartier dishes, such as beef, lamb or steak recipes, tend to pair well with more flavourful medium or full-bodied red wines.

Some wines will happily span two or more courses (for example, a starter and main course or a main course and a cheese course), while others are best suited to just one course.

So, when matching wine with food, the main things to consider include the intensity of flavour and richness of the food, as well as the body or weight of the wine. The body and weight of the wine can be light, medium or full-bodied (the alcohol level of the wine being the main contributor to the wine's body – alcohol gives wine its viscosity and consequent mouth feel).

You should also consider the acidity of the wine (and the food), the tannins in the wine (tannins are most commonly found in red wines) and the sweetness of white wine (and the food).

It is important that you serve wine at the correct temperature to fully enjoy all the aromas and flavours at their best. Generally speaking, white, rosé and sparkling wines are best served chilled and red wines are better at room temperature, but there are exceptions to these rules and it's partly down to personal taste too. Some lighter-bodied reds, for example, may be preferred slightly chilled. Check the label to see what is advised for the wine you are serving. A standard bottle of wine will serve around four to six people.

If you've chosen a red wine to go with your meal, be sure to let it breathe at room temperature before serving. You can do this by opening the bottle (and ideally pouring it into a wine decanter) about an hour or so before serving. Make sure that white, rosé and sparkling wines are served well chilled. It could also be an idea to keep an ice bucket or wine chiller close to hand to keep the wine perfectly cold and to avoid having to go back and forth to the refrigerator during the meal. Make sure you keep a corkscrew handy as well, plus a wine bottle stopper or two to 're-cork' open bottles.

If the time is right to bring on the bubbles, there's no better way to set the tone for a special meal than by popping open a bottle of fizz. The three top choices are Champagne, Cava or Prosecco, although there are other interesting alternatives. Champagne is the premier fizz of the three, but also the priciest, with Cava and Prosecco offering good sparkling alternatives for those on a slightly less expensive budget.

For non-wine drinkers, chilled beers and lagers are good alternatives, as are ciders and spirits. There are also non-alcoholic wines and beers for those who prefer not to drink alcohol or designated drivers. A jug of iced tap water or mineral water on the table is a welcome addition too.

# Roasted Fig Tartlets with Crème de Cassis & Honey Mascarpone

Crème de cassis syrup and ripe fresh figs combine beautifully on top of these crisp puff pastry tartlets. Served with sumptuous honey mascarpone, these create the ideal indulgent desserts, guaranteed to satisfy all those with a sweet tooth.

**SERVES 6**

Prepares in 45–50 minutes,

zest and juice of 1 orange

2 tbsp clear honey

100 ml/3½ fl oz crème de cassis

12 ripe black figs

flour, for dusting

500 g/1 lb 2 oz puff pastry

150 g/5½ oz butter

150 g/5½ oz caster sugar

150 g/5½ oz ground almonds

2 egg yolks

icing sugar, for dusting

### Honey Mascarpone

300 g/10½ oz mascarpone cheese

2 tbsp natural yogurt or crème fraîche

3 tbsp clear honey

1 vanilla pod, split in half, seeds removed

1. Preheat the oven to 180°C/350°F/Gas Mark 4. In a small saucepan, mix the orange juice and honey and bring to the boil. Cook for about 10 minutes, or until reduced and syrupy, then add the crème de cassis. Halve the figs and place in the pan. Spoon over the cassis mixture so that they are well coated. Remove the pan from the heat.

2. Flour a board and roll the pastry out on the board to a thickness of 5 mm/¼ inch. Using a saucer as a template, cut out six rounds and place them on squares of baking paper. Using a fork, prick lots of holes in the centre of the rounds, leaving a clean border of 2 cm/¾ inch around the edge of each round. Place the rounds in the refrigerator for 20 minutes, then transfer them to the preheated oven and bake for 10 minutes.

3. Meanwhile, cream the butter and sugar in a food processor until smooth and pale, add the ground almonds and orange zest and combine. Add the egg yolks and a tablespoon of the soaking juice from the figs, then mix until smooth.

4. When the pastry cases are a pale golden colour, spoon some of the almond mixture into the centre of each. With the back of the spoon, spread the mixture up to the border, where the pastry will have risen more. Spoon four fig halves onto each tart and then spoon some of the cassis syrup on top.

5. Reduce the oven temperature to 160°C/325°F/Gas Mark 3, transfer the tarts to the oven and bake for 12 minutes, or until the mixture is set and the base of the pastry is crisp and golden brown. Reduce any leftover cassis liquid by simmering until thick and syrupy. Take the tarts out of the oven and spoon some of the hot syrup over the fruit.

6. To make the honey mascarpone, place the mascarpone cheese in a bowl and whisk together with the yogurt, honey and the vanilla seeds. Whisk until smooth. Dust the tartlets with icing sugar and serve with the mascarpone immediately.

# Hot Chocolate Desserts & Candied Oranges

Chocolate and orange are a match made in heaven and no more so than with these mouth-watering molten-centred baked chocolate puddings served with candied oranges. For committed chocoholics, this decadent chocolate dessert will really hit the spot.

SERVES 6
Prepares in 55 minutes,
 plus cooling
Cooks in 1 hour 10 minutes

125 g/4½ oz 70% plain chocolate,
  broken into pieces
85 g/3 oz unsalted butter,
  plus extra for greasing
2 cloves
2 cardamom pods
¼ tsp ground cinnamon
¼ tsp ground nutmeg
zest of 1 large orange
2 large eggs
2 large egg yolks
3 tbsp caster sugar
75 g/2¾ oz plain flour,
  plus extra for dusting

### Candied Orange Peel
5 oranges
500 ml/18 fl oz water
8 cardamom pods
2 cinnamon sticks
2 cloves
½ tsp grated nutmeg
300 g/10½ oz caster sugar

1. Preheat the oven to 220°C/425°F/Gas Mark 7. Lightly butter and flour six 6-cm/2½-inch ramekins.

2. Place the chocolate and the butter in a heatproof bowl set over a saucepan of simmering water. Stir regularly to ensure an even texture.

3. In a pestle and mortar, crush the cloves and the cardamom pods, add the cinnamon and the nutmeg, then sift to a fine powder. When the chocolate is melted, remove from the heat and leave to cool. Stir in the ground spices and orange zest.

4. In a separate bowl, whisk the eggs, egg yolks and the caster sugar until the eggs are pale and mousse-like. Fold in the melted chocolate and the flour.

5. Pour the chocolate mixture into the prepared ramekins and bake in the preheated oven for 8–10 minutes. The centres of the puddings should be runny.

6. Meanwhile, make the candied orange peel. Remove the peel and pith of the oranges with a sharp knife. Cut into the flesh while doing this so that each piece consists of peel, pith and about 5 mm/¼ inch of flesh. You can eat the rest of the orange or save it for another dish.

7. While you are cutting the fruit, reserve the juice in a saucepan. Place the pieces of orange in the saucepan with the orange juice and cover with the water.

8. Bring to a simmer and allow to cook gently for 30 minutes, or until the liquid has reduced by one third.

9. Using a pestle and mortar, crush the cardamom pods and discard the tough green shells. Add the seeds to the pan with the other spices and the sugar. Stir in the sugar to dissolve and then continue to boil the oranges for about 30 minutes. Leave to cool, then cut the peel into slivers and set aside until ready to serve. Reserve the syrup.

10. To serve, run a small knife around the inside of each ramekin, gently turn out into the palm of your hand and then plate on individual plates. Serve with the candied oranges and some of the reserved syrup.

# Mocha Soufflés with Mascarpone

*If you are looking to create a simple but sophisticated dinner party dessert, these individual towering baked soufflés are easy to make, but remember to serve them straight from the oven as soon as they are cooked.*

**SERVES 4**
Prepares in 25–30 minutes,
  plus cooling
Cooks in 18–20 minutes

*2 tsp butter, to grease*
*2 tbsp ground almonds*
*1 tbsp cocoa powder,*
  *plus a little extra to dust*
*1 tbsp strong espresso*
*small pinch of sea salt*
*5 tbsp cold water*
*3 egg whites*
*1 tbsp rice malt syrup*
*4 tbsp mascarpone cheese, to serve*

1. Preheat the oven to 190°C/375°F/ Gas Mark 5. Lightly grease four ramekins, then sprinkle with the ground almonds. Roll and rotate the ramekins so the almonds stick to the butter, coating all sides.

2. Put the cocoa powder, espresso, salt and water in a small saucepan and cook, stirring over a low heat, until smooth. Increase the heat to medium–high and bring to the boil, then cook for a further minute. Pour the mixture into a large bowl and leave to cool.

3. Put the egg whites in a separate large, clean glass bowl and whisk until they form soft peaks. Add the rice malt syrup and whisk again until you have stiff peaks. Using a metal spoon, gently fold a spoonful of the egg white into the cocoa mixture, preserving as much air as possible, then fold in the rest.

4. Spoon the mixture into the prepared ramekins. Bake in the preheated oven for 10–12 minutes, or until the soufflés are towering out of the ramekins.

5. Add a tablespoon of the mascarpone to each ramekin and sprinkle with the cocoa powder. Serve immediately, as quickly as possible before the soufflés start to collapse.

# Spiced Plum & Blackberry Brulées

*These all-time favourite rich and indulgent desserts are given a tempting twist with a lovely mix of lightly cooked autumnal fruits hidden beneath the luscious creamy layer on top. Perfect for a special seasonal sweet treat.*

**SERVES 6**
Prepares in 25 minutes,
 plus cooling and chilling
Cooks in 14–15 minutes

*300 g/10½ oz plums, stoned and sliced*
*175 g/6 oz blackberries*
*2 tbsp water*
*¼ tsp ground cinnamon*
*5 tbsp light muscovado sugar*
*225 ml/8 fl oz double cream*
*225 g/8 oz Greek-style natural yogurt*

1. Put the plums, blackberries and water in a saucepan. Sprinkle over the cinnamon and 2 tablespoons of the sugar, then cover and cook over a medium–low heat for 10 minutes, or until just tender. Leave to cool.

2. Put the cream in a large bowl and whisk until soft swirls form, then fold in the yogurt.

3. Spoon the fruit and a little of the juice from the pan into six ovenproof 175-ml/6-fl oz ramekins or soufflé dishes. Dot teaspoons of the cream mixture over the top, then spread it into an even layer. Chill for at least 30 minutes.

4. Sprinkle the remaining 3 tablespoons of sugar over the tops of the dishes. Stand them in the base of the grill pan, pack ice around them to keep them cold and grill for 4–5 minutes, or until the sugar has dissolved and caramelized. Leave to cool for 2 minutes, then serve immediately.

# Goat's Cheese with Honey & Walnuts

*Goat's cheese served simply with honey and walnuts makes a surprisingly appetizing combination, ideal for serving after a rich meal. For a fresh and fruity touch, add a few fresh pear slices to each serving too.*

**SERVES 4**
Prepares in 10–15 minutes
No cooking

*about 175 g/6 oz good quality goat's cheese, such as Monte Enebro, in one piece*
*about 115 g/4 oz clear honey, such as orange-blossom or thyme-flavoured*
*100 g/3½ oz walnut halves, chopped*

1. Remove the cheese from the refrigerator at least 20 minutes before serving, to allow it to come up to room temperature.

2. Pour the honey into a bowl. Place the walnuts in another bowl.

3. Serve the goat's cheese on a cheese board with a cheese knife and let everyone cut a slice for themselves. Drizzle over some honey, with a dipper, if available, and sprinkle with chopped walnuts.

4. Alternatively, cut the cheese into four quarters and place a slice on each of four serving plates. Drizzle over some honey, sprinkle with chopped nuts and serve.

# Champagne Sorbet

*This elegant frozen dessert provides a really refreshing palate cleanser or luscious light dessert after an indulgent meal. Make it ahead of time, then simply soften it slightly and scoop when you are ready to serve.*

**SERVES 4**
Prepares in 15–20 minutes,
 plus cooling and churning
 or freezing
Cooks in 5–7 minutes

*juice of 1 lemon*
*200 ml/7 fl oz water*
*150 g/5½ oz granulated sugar*
*1 tbsp liquid glucose*
*250 ml/9 fl oz Champagne*
*mint leaves or elderflower sprigs,*
 *to decorate*

1. Combine all the ingredients except the Champagne in a small saucepan. Place the saucepan over a low heat and stir gently until all the sugar has dissolved. Increase the heat and bring to the boil, then remove from the heat. Leave to cool to room temperature.

2. When cool, add the Champagne and stir in. If using an ice-cream maker, pour into the ice-cream maker and churn for 30–45 minutes, or according to the manufacturer's instructions.

3. Alternatively, freeze the mixture in a freezerproof container, uncovered, for 1–2 hours, or until mushy. Turn the mixture into a bowl and stir vigorously to break down any ice crystals. Return the sorbet to the container and freeze for a further 2–3 hours, or until firm. Cover the container with a lid for storing.

4. When ready to serve, leave the sorbet to soften slightly at room temperature before serving in sundae dishes, decorated with a few mint leaves.

### Martini
*Shaken, not stirred!*

### Champagne Sidecar
*A great alternative to Buck's Fizz.*

### Long Island Iced Tea
*Classic and refreshing.*

### Black Velvet
*For beer and wine lovers alike.*

# Martini

SERVES 1
Prepares in 10 minutes
No cooking

4–6 cracked ice cubes
3 measures gin
1 tsp dry vermouth, or to taste
cocktail olive, to decorate

1. Put the cracked ice cubes into a cocktail shaker.

2. Pour the gin and vermouth over the ice cubes.

3. Shake until well frosted. Strain into a chilled cocktail glass.

4. Decorate with the olive. Serve immediately.

---

# Champagne Sidecar

SERVES 1
Prepares in 10 minutes
No cooking

1½ measures bourbon
1 measure Cointreau
¼ measure lemon juice
ice
chilled Champagne

1. Shake the bourbon, Cointreau and lemon juice over ice and strain into a chilled flute.

2. Top up the flute with chilled Champagne and serve immediately.

# Long Island Iced Tea

SERVES 1
Prepares in 12 minutes
No cooking

cracked ice
1 measure vodka
1 measure gin
1 measure white tequila
1 measure white rum
½ measure white crème de menthe
2 measures lemon juice
1 tsp caster sugar
cola
lime wedge, to decorate

1. Put 4–6 cracked ice cubes into a cocktail shaker. Pour all the liquid ingredients except the cola over the ice, add the sugar and shake vigorously until well frosted.

2. Half fill a tall glass with cracked ice and strain over the cocktail.

3. Top up with cola, decorate with the lime wedge and serve immediately.

---

# Black Velvet

SERVES 1
Prepares in 5 minutes
No cooking

stout, chilled
sparkling white wine, chilled

1. Half fill a tumbler with stout, then very slowly pour in an equal quantity of wine over the back of a spoon that is just touching the top of the stout and the edge of the glass. Serve immediately.

# Sunday Best Ever Brunch

---

*Sunday brunch is the perfect excuse to enjoy some tasty, laid-back food. This is the time for kicking back and relaxing as you enter the most chilled day of the weekend. Brunch food reflects this relaxed vibe, as it provides maximum enjoyment for a minimum of culinary effort. There's only one day left until work on Monday so make the most of it!*

---

*Sunday morning is all about lounging around and enjoying a long and lazy brunch. Once you get up, grind some fresh beans and get some espresso on the go, as nothing should be attempted before a leisurely cup of coffee. Then settle down with the papers for a while, before starting to think about what delicious brunch dish you can throw together.*

If you have a juicer or citrus press, you might want to squeeze some fresh fruit or vegetable juice and keep it chilled, ready to enjoy a bit later, or bring out the blender and create a simple smoothie to boost your energy while you cook.

In this chapter, the focus is firmly on a super selection of mouth-watering dishes, perfect for getting the taste buds going and all certain to deliver on flavour and appeal. These are relaxed and informal fuss-free meals that don't require too much effort, but that will satisfy those who enjoy something a bit more substantial to start the day. We include flavour-packed egg scrambles, pancakes, platters, pies, tarts and frittatas, all promising to hit the right spot on this most chilled-out of mornings.

Superb staples include Spinach Scrambled Eggs and Eggs Florentine, plus other delicious eats like Avocado, Bacon & Chilli Frittata or Mini Salmon & Broccoli Pies. For vegetable lovers, the Savoury Vegetable Pancakes are sure to appeal to more adventurous eaters or those looking for something substantial to eat.

If you are in a celebratory mood or you are planning a really lazy afternoon, then why not try some tempting cocktail quenchers, such as classics like Mint Julep or Bloody Mary, or the more decadent Champagne Cocktail.

Many of these recipes can be knocked up without much effort and some can be prepared ahead too, making for easy eating on a Sunday morning. Depending on the number of guests joining you

for brunch, why not make a selection of dishes and let people just dig in and help themselves? The Wholewheat Spinach, Pea & Feta Tart or the No-crust Squash, Chorizo & Goat's Cheese Quiche can both be made ahead. All that you will need to accompany these dishes is slices of fresh crusty bread or freshly made toast or some freshly baked croissants. Or, you could try some crispy crackers, a block of good quality butter and a jar or two of home-made chutney or pickle.

On the other hand, if it's just a quiet weekend, why not indulge yourself and serve brunch in bed? It couldn't be easier to relax and while away the morning with this delicious selection of feel-good brunch favourites. What better way could there surely be to start your sleepy Sunday? The stresses of the working week could not be further away...

# Spinach Scrambled Eggs with Wholegrain Rye Toast

*It's hard to beat scrambled eggs served with hot, crispy wholegrain toast for brunch, but lightly cooked spinach and a seasoning of nutmeg add extra flavour and appeal to this classic dish.*

**SERVES 4**
Prepares in 15–20 minutes
Cooks in 9–12 minutes

*200 g/7 oz baby spinach, chopped*
*8 large eggs*
*3 tbsp milk*
*15 g/½ oz unsalted butter*
*4 slices of wholegrain rye bread*
*pinch of freshly grated nutmeg*
*salt and pepper*

1. Place a large frying pan over a high heat. Add the spinach and cook in the water still clinging to it from washing, stirring for 1–2 minutes or until the leaves have just wilted. Transfer it to a sieve and squeeze out as much of the moisture as possible. Keep warm.

2. Crack the eggs into a bowl, add the milk and season with salt and pepper. Beat lightly with a fork until evenly mixed.

3. Melt the butter in the frying pan over a medium heat. Pour in the eggs and cook, stirring, for 5–6 minutes, or until they are just beginning to set. Add the spinach and cook, stirring, for 2–3 minutes, or until the eggs are lightly set.

4. Meanwhile, lightly toast the rye bread, then cut each slice in half.

5. Spoon the spinach scramble over the toast, sprinkle with nutmeg and serve immediately.

# Eggs Florentine

*This superb egg-based staple is great for those who enjoy something a bit more substantial to start the day. Serve it bubbling hot from the oven and get stuck in.*

**SERVES 4**
Prepares in 15–20 minutes
Cooks in 15–20 minutes

*1 tbsp olive oil*
*200 g/7 oz baby spinach*
*4 thick slices ciabatta bread*
*25 g/1 oz butter*
*4 large eggs*
*100 g/3½ oz Cheddar cheese, grated*
*salt and pepper*
*freshly grated nutmeg, to serve*

1. Preheat the grill to high. Heat the oil in a wok or large saucepan, add the spinach and stir-fry for 2–3 minutes, or until the leaves are wilted. Drain in a colander, season to taste with salt and pepper and keep warm.

2. Toast the bread on both sides until golden. Spread one side of each slice with butter and place buttered side up in a baking dish.

3. Bring a small saucepan of lightly salted water to the boil, crack the eggs into the water and poach for about 3 minutes, or until the whites are set but the yolks still runny. Remove from the pan with a slotted spoon.

4. Arrange the spinach on the toast and top each slice with a poached egg. Sprinkle with the grated cheese. Cook under the preheated grill for 1–2 minutes until the cheese has melted. Sprinkle with nutmeg and serve immediately.

# Courgette Rösti with Smoked Salmon & Eggs

*Individual pan-fried courgette rösti, topped with thin slices of smoked salmon and creamy scrambled eggs makes a mouth-watering combination, creating the perfect choice for a lazy, leisurely Sunday brunch for two.*

**SERVES 2**
Prepares in 25 minutes
Cooks in 12–16 minutes

3 large eggs
1 tbsp double cream
2 tsp finely snipped fresh chives
15 g/½ oz butter
2 large slices of smoked salmon, to serve
salt and pepper

## Rösti

300 g/10½ oz courgette, grated
2 tsp quinoa flour
20 g/¾ oz Parmesan cheese, grated
1 large egg yolk
1 tbsp double cream
1 tbsp vegetable oil

1. Preheat the oven to 110°C/225°F/ Gas Mark ¼. To make the rösti, lay a clean tea towel on a work surface and pile the courgette in the centre. Holding the tea towel over the sink, gather the sides together and twist them tightly until all the liquid from the courgette has run out.

2. Put the courgette, flour, Parmesan, egg yolk and cream in a bowl and mix well. Roll the mixture into two balls and flatten them with the palms of your hands to make thick patties.

3. Heat the oil in a small frying pan over a medium–low heat. Cook the röstis for 5–8 minutes on each side, or until golden brown. Remove from the heat, transfer to a baking sheet and put them in the oven to keep warm.

4. To make the scrambled eggs, crack the eggs into a bowl, add the cream and chives and season with salt and pepper. Beat with a fork until evenly mixed.

5. Wipe the frying pan clean with kitchen paper, then melt the butter in the pan over a low heat. Pour in the egg mixture and cook, stirring, for 5–6 minutes, or until the eggs are just set.

6. Put the warm röstis on two plates. Spoon the scrambled eggs over them, then top with the salmon. Grind over some black pepper and serve immediately.

# Yam, Swede & Mushroom Hash

For something that little bit different, entice your guests to the table with this delicious pan-fried hash recipe that uses yams and swedes instead of potatoes. Serve it straight from the pan and all tuck in.

**SERVES 4**

Prepares in 20–25 minutes
Cooks in 25–30 minutes

3 tbsp olive oil
500 g/1 lb 2 oz yams, diced
280 g/10 oz swedes, diced
1 onion, chopped
175 g/6 oz streaky bacon,
  sliced, or lardons
250 g/9 oz mushrooms, sliced
4 eggs
salt and pepper
chopped fresh flat-leaf parsley, to garnish

1. Heat the oil in a large, lidded frying pan over a high heat. Add the yams and swedes to the pan, stir in the oil to coat and season to taste generously with salt and pepper. Cook, stirring occasionally, for 10–15 minutes, or until all of the vegetables are just turning golden and soft.

2. Add the chopped onion and bacon to the frying pan. Stir everything well and continue to cook for 5 minutes, or until the onion is soft and the bacon is cooked. Add the mushrooms to the pan, stir and cover the pan. Cook the mixture for a further 5 minutes.

3. Make four indentations in the mixture and carefully break an egg into each one. Cover the pan and cook for a further 3–4 minutes, or until the egg whites are firm but the yolks are still soft.

4. Transfer the hash to four warmed plates. Garnish each serving with the chopped parsley and serve immediately.

# Antipasti Meat Platter

*The simplicity of this dish is very appealing as it looks great and everyone can just help themselves. Assemble the platter a little ahead of time if you like, then serve it when you are all ready to eat.*

**SERVES 4**
Prepares in 20–25 minutes
No cooking

*1 cantaloupe melon*
*55 g/2 oz Italian salami, thinly sliced*
*8 slices prosciutto*
*8 slices bresaola*
*8 slices mortadella*
*4 plum tomatoes, thinly sliced*
*4 fresh figs, quartered*

*55 g/2 oz black olives, stoned*
*2 tbsp shredded fresh basil leaves*
*4 tbsp extra virgin olive oil,*
  *plus extra to serve*
*pepper*
*sliced ciabatta loaf, to serve*

1. Cut the melon in half, scoop out and discard the seeds, then cut the flesh into wedges. Arrange the wedges on one half of a large serving platter.

2. Arrange the salami, prosciutto, bresaola and mortadella in loose folds on the other half of the platter. Arrange the tomato slices and fig quarters along the centre of the platter.

3. Sprinkle the olives and basil over the platter and drizzle with oil. Season to taste with pepper, then serve with slices of ciabatta and extra oil, for dipping and drizzling.

# Wholewheat Spinach, Pea & Feta Tart

*A seasonal star of the summer kitchen, those opting for a meat-free day will savour the flavours of this very tempting vegetable and feta cheese tart. Serve it simply with some peppery salad leaves.*

**SERVES 6**

Prepares in 35 minutes,
  plus chilling and cooling
Cooks in 1–1¼ hours

15 g/½ oz unsalted butter
3 spring onions, thinly sliced
200 g/7 oz baby spinach
100 g/3½ oz podded peas
3 eggs
250 ml/9 fl oz milk
100 g/3½ oz feta cheese, drained
  and finely crumbled

115 g/4 oz cherry tomatoes
salt and pepper

## Pastry

115 g/4 oz unsalted butter, cut into cubes
225 g/8 oz wholemeal plain flour,
  plus extra for dusting
2 eggs, beaten

1. To make the pastry, put the butter and flour in a mixing bowl and season with salt and pepper. Rub the butter into the flour until it resembles fine crumbs. Gradually mix in enough egg to make a soft but not sticky dough.

2. Lightly dust a work surface with flour. Knead the pastry gently, then roll it out on the surface to a little larger than a 25-cm/10-inch loose-bottomed flan tin. Lift the pastry over the rolling pin, ease it into the tin and press it into the sides. Trim the pastry so that it stands a little above the top of the tin, then prick the base with a fork.

3. Cover the tart case with clingfilm and chill in the refrigerator for 15–30 minutes. Meanwhile, preheat the oven to 190°C/375°F/Gas Mark 5.

4. To make the filling, melt the butter in a frying pan over a medium heat. Add the spring onions and cook for 2–3 minutes, or until softened. Add the spinach, turn the heat to high, and cook, stirring, until wilted. Set aside to cool.

5. Cook the peas in a small saucepan of boiling water for 2 minutes. Drain, then plunge into iced water and drain again. Crack the eggs into a jug, add the milk, season with salt and pepper and beat with a fork.

6. Line the tart case with baking paper and baking beans and place on a baking sheet. Bake for 10 minutes, then remove the paper and beans and bake for 5 minutes more, or until the base of the tart is crisp and dry.

7. Drain any cooking juices from the spinach mixture into the eggs. Put the mixture in the tart case, add the peas, then sprinkle over the cheese. Fork the eggs and milk together once more, then pour into the tart case and dot the tomatoes over the top. Bake for 40–50 minutes, or until set and golden. Leave to cool for 20 minutes, then serve.

# Avocado, Bacon & Chilli Frittata

*A firm favourite when it comes to brunch, frittatas are great for sharing. Avocados add an appealing taste twist and texture to this flavourful frittata, with fresh chilli and lime juice adding a final bit of zing.*

**SERVES 4**
Prepares in 20–25 minutes
Cooks in 12–17 minutes

1 tbsp vegetable oil
8 streaky bacon rashers, roughly chopped
6 eggs, beaten
3 tbsp double cream
2 large avocados, sliced
1 red chilli, deseeded and thinly sliced
½ lime
salt and pepper

1. Preheat the grill to medium. Heat the oil in a 20-cm/8-inch ovenproof frying pan over a medium heat. Add the bacon and fry, stirring, for 4–5 minutes, or until crisp and golden. Using a slotted spoon, transfer to a plate lined with kitchen paper. Remove the pan from the heat.

2. Pour the eggs into a bowl, add the cream and season with salt and pepper, then beat. Return the pan to the heat. When it is hot, pour in the egg mixture and cook for 1–2 minutes, without stirring. Sprinkle the bacon and avocado on top and cook for a further 2–3 minutes, or until the frittata is almost set and the underside is golden brown.

3. Place the frittata under the grill and cook for 3–4 minutes, or until the top is golden brown and the egg is set. Scatter with the chilli and squeeze over the lime juice. Cut into wedges and serve.

# Savoury Vegetable Pancakes with Pesto & Braised Spinach

Home-made pesto is hard to beat and it combines beautifully with the béchamel sauce and braised spinach in this recipe. Served with crisply cooked home-made pancakes, this is sure to be a hit with any guests.

SERVES 6
Prepares in 50 minutes,
 plus cooling
Cooks in 50–55 minutes

275 ml/9½ fl oz ready-made
  Béchamel sauce
olive oil, for frying
rocket leaves, to serve

### Pancake Batter
300 g/10½ oz plain flour
2 egg yolks
2 tbsp olive oil
500 ml/18 fl oz milk
salt and pepper

### Pesto
3 tbsp pine nuts
2 large garlic cloves
½ tsp coarse salt

2 bunches of fresh basil
60 g/2¼ oz freshly grated
  Parmesan cheese
125 ml/4 fl oz olive oil
juice of ½ lemon

### Braised Spinach
1 tbsp extra virgin olive oil
1 garlic clove,
  finely sliced lengthways
250 g/9 oz baby spinach
a splash of lemon juice
salt and pepper

1. Preheat the oven to 190°C/375°F/Gas Mark 5. For the pesto, roast the pine nuts on a baking tray for 3–4 minutes, or until golden brown. Crush the garlic with the salt, using the side of a heavy knife. Using a pestle and mortar, crush the garlic and the pine nuts to a rough paste. Roughly chop the basil and then add to the pestle and mortar a handful at a time. Continue to pound until you have a smooth paste, then stir in the grated Parmesan cheese.

2. Gradually add the olive oil and the lemon juice and season with salt and pepper. Use immediately or store in an airtight container in the refrigerator.

3. For the spinach, heat the olive oil in a large, heavy-based saucepan or wok. Fry the garlic until it is a pale golden colour. Add all the spinach to the hot oil. Cover with a lid and cook for about 2 minutes, or until the leaves are wilted. Shake well and remove the lid. Stir to ensure all the leaves are wilted. Drain off any excess water and liquid. Season with salt and pepper, and a splash of lemon juice. Mix together.

4. Mix the pesto with the Béchamel sauce and then stir into the spinach. Adjust the seasoning.

5. To make the pancake batter, sift the flour into a large bowl and make a well in the centre. Place the egg yolks in the well. Add some salt and pepper and the olive oil. Whisk together until everything is thoroughly combined. Whisk in the milk until you have a smooth batter.

6. Heat a non-stick frying pan or an omelette pan. When hot, add a little olive oil, then pour out the excess. Use a ladle to pour some batter into the hot pan. Lift the pan and move it around so the batter covers the base of the pan. Tip the excess batter back into the bowl.

7. Cook the pancake over a medium–high heat for about 1–2 minutes, or until the underside is crisp and golden brown in colour. Using a palette knife, turn the pancake and cook on the other side. When completely cooked, remove the pancake from the pan and leave to cool on some kitchen paper, to soak up any oil. Repeat the process, making pancakes and leaving them to cool on the paper, until all the batter has been used. Preheat the oven to 180°C/350°F/Gas Mark 4.

8. When the pancakes have cooled, lay them out and spread the pesto and spinach mixture in a thick dollop in the centre of the pancakes. Fold in the two sides and then roll them like a cigar.

9. Arrange the stuffed pancakes in an ovenproof dish, place in the preheated oven and bake for 8–10 minutes. Serve the pancakes immediately, with the rocket on the side.

# No-crust Squash, Chorizo & Goat's Cheese Quiche

Roasted butternut squash and spicy chorizo team up in this creamy baked quiche that is sure to get taste buds going as the delicious aromas waft from the oven. This is an excellent brunch dish for sharing.

**SERVES 4**
Prepares in 35 minutes,
  plus chilling and cooling
Cooks in 1 hour 20 minutes

400 g/14 oz butternut squash flesh, diced
1 tbsp olive oil
200 g/7 oz chorizo, cut into
  small, irregular chunks
3 eggs
100 ml/3½ fl oz crème fraîche
2 tbsp fresh thyme leaves
100 g/3½ oz semi-hard goat's cheese
salt and pepper
green salad leaves, to serve (optional)

## Pastry

50 g/1¾ oz cold butter, diced
100 g/3½ oz wholemeal plain flour,
  plus extra for dusting
2 tbsp cold water

1. Preheat the oven to 190°C/375°F/Gas Mark 5.

2. To make the pastry, put the butter in a mixing bowl, add the flour and season with salt and pepper. Rub the butter into the flour until it resembles fine breadcrumbs. Alternatively, process it in a food processor. Gradually mix in enough of the water to make a soft, but not sticky, dough.

3. Lightly dust a work surface with flour. Pat the dough into a disc, then wrap it tightly in clingfilm. Chill in the refrigerator for at least 30 minutes.

4. Meanwhile, to make the filling, put the butternut squash and oil into a large roasting tin, season with salt and pepper and toss well.

5. Roast in the preheated oven for 15 minutes, then stir and add the chorizo. Roast for 15 minutes more, or until the squash is crisp on the edges and tender, and the chorizo is crisp. Set aside to cool.

6. Dust the work surface with more flour. Knead the pastry gently, then roll it out to a circle that is just under 23 cm/9 inches in diameter. Place on a baking sheet and prick all over with a fork.

7. Bake in the preheated oven for 20 minutes. Remove from the oven and, using the base of a 20-cm/8-inch loose-bottomed tart tin as a template, cut a circle in the pastry. Set aside to cool.

8. Meanwhile, crack the eggs into a large bowl and lightly beat with a fork. Stir in the crème fraîche and thyme and season with plenty of pepper.

9. Reduce the oven temperature to 160°C/325°F/Gas Mark 3. Line the 20-cm/8-inch tart tin with baking paper.

10. Carefully place your cooled pastry circle in the tin, then scatter with the chorizo and butternut squash. Pour over the egg mixture, then crumble the goat's cheese on top.

11. Bake the quiche in the preheated oven for 30 minutes, or until the egg in the centre is set.

12. Serve the quiche warm or at room temperature and with salad leaves on the side, if using.

# Mini Salmon & Broccoli Pies

*Show off your pastry-making skills with these ultimate individual golden baked pies. These tasty treats are perfect for Sunday brunch with friends.*

## MAKES 8
Prepares in 35 minutes,
 plus cooling and chilling
Cooks in 40–45 minutes

### Filling

125 g/4½ oz broccoli florets
125 g/4½ oz salmon fillet
25 g/1 oz butter
25 g/1 oz plain flour
275 ml/9½ fl oz warm milk
salt and pepper
salad, to serve

### Pastry

225 g/8 oz plain flour,
 plus extra for dusting
pinch of salt
115 g/4 oz butter
about 3 tbsp iced water
1 egg, lightly beaten with
 1 tbsp water

1. Cook the broccoli in lightly salted boiling water for 5–10 minutes, or until tender. Drain and leave to cool. Meanwhile, bring a saucepan of lightly salted water to the boil, then reduce the heat to very low. Add the fish and poach, turning once, for 5 minutes, or until the flesh flakes easily. Remove from the pan and leave to cool.

2. Melt the butter in a small saucepan, add the flour and cook over a low heat, stirring constantly, for 2 minutes. Gradually stir in the warm milk. Bring to the boil, stirring constantly, then simmer, stirring, until thickened and smooth. Season to taste, remove from the heat and leave to cool, stirring occasionally.

3. Meanwhile, to make the pastry, sift the flour and salt into a bowl. Add the butter and cut into the flour. Rub in with your fingertips until the mixture resembles breadcrumbs. Stir in the water and mix to a smooth dough.

4. Shape the pastry into a ball, cover and chill for 30 minutes.

5. Remove the skin and flake the flesh of the fish into a bowl. Break up the broccoli florets and add to the bowl. Stir in the white sauce and season to taste. Mix well.

6. Preheat the oven to 200°C/400°F/Gas Mark 6. Roll out the pastry on a lightly floured surface and stamp out 16 rounds with a 10-cm/4-inch cutter. Put 8 rounds into a muffin tin. Add spoonfuls of the salmon mixture without filling the pastry cases completely. Brush the edges of the remaining rounds with water and use to cover the pies, pressing with the tines of a fork to seal.

7. Brush the tops with the beaten egg mixture and bake for 20–25 minutes, or until golden brown. Serve with salad.

### Fresh Lemonade
*Perfect on a summer's morning.*

### Champagne Cocktail
*A relaxing start to a Sunday.*

### Mint Julep
*A refreshing cocktail for a brunch with friends.*

### Bloody Mary
*The ultimate brunch companion.*

# Fresh Lemonade

SERVES 6
Prepares in 20 minutes, plus standing
No cooking

*4 large lemons, preferably unwaxed*
*175 g/6 oz caster sugar*
*850 ml/1½ pints boiling water*
*ice cubes*

1. Scrub the lemons well, then dry. Using a vegetable peeler, peel three of the lemons very thinly. Place the peel in a large jug or basin, add the sugar and boiling water and stir well until the sugar has dissolved. Cover the jug and leave to stand for at least 3 hours, stirring occasionally. Meanwhile, squeeze the juice from the 3 lemons and reserve.

2. Remove and discard the lemon peel and stir in the reserved lemon juice. Thinly slice the remaining lemon and cut the slices in half. Add to the lemonade together with the ice cubes. Stir and serve immediately.

---

# Champagne Cocktail

SERVES 1
Prepares in 10 minutes
No cooking

*1 sugar cube*
*2 dashes Angostura bitters*
*1 measure brandy*
*Champagne, chilled*

1. Place the sugar cube in the bottom of a chilled flute. Add the bitters and the brandy.

2. Top up with Champagne and serve immediately.

# Mint Julep

SERVES 1
Prepares in 10 minutes
No cooking

*1 fresh mint sprig, plus extra to decorate*
*1 tbsp sugar syrup*
*cracked ice*
*3 measures bourbon*

1. Strip the leaves from the mint sprig and put in a small chilled glass.

2. Crush the mint leaves and pour in the sugar syrup.

3. Half-fill the glass with cracked ice and stir. Add the bourbon and decorate with the remaining mint sprig. Serve immediately.

---

# Bloody Mary

SERVES 1
Prepares in 10 minutes
No cooking

*4–6 cracked ice cubes*
*dash hot pepper sauce*
*dash Worcestershire sauce*
*2 measures vodka*
*6 measures tomato juice*
*juice of ½ lemon*
*pinch celery salt*
*pinch cayenne pepper*
*celery stick and lemon slice, to decorate*

1. Put the ice into a cocktail shaker. Dash the hot pepper sauce and Worcestershire sauce over the ice.

2. Add the vodka, tomato and lemon juices and shake vigorously. Strain into a tall glass, add the celery salt and cayenne and decorate with the celery and lemon.

# Sunday Long & Lazy Lunches

Sunday is the ideal time over the weekend to invite friends or family round and enjoy a long and lazy lunch together. This chapter is all about creating delicious dishes that really pack a flavour punch, without being overly fussy or fastidious. Be it for a special occasion, a celebratory meal, or simply an excuse for a culinary blowout, these meals provide the perfect opportunity to gather guests round the table and tempt them with some superb standout dishes.

*Sunday morning often affords you a bit more scope in the kitchen, making it the prime time to prepare a feast of flavours for your companions. Long, slow roasts in particular lend themselves to Sunday lunch dining, because you can take your time to make the meal while talking with friends as you cook. Delicious dishes like paellas and stews that need a little more attention during cooking are ideal for Sunday lunch entertaining too, allowing you to get the best out of the food you love to prepare.*

To whet the appetite, kick things off with a tasty array of assorted small bites to munch on and to accompany a selection of chilled drinks or aperitifs. Once your guests are relaxed and ready to eat, select a simple but stylish starter that everyone can tuck into, like Parma ham and fresh figs, blinis with smoked salmon, a tasty pâté or a beautiful baked camembert cheese, making sure you leave plenty of room for the main event.

Next up, it's time to show off your culinary prowess and wow your guests with a magnificent main course. We feature an appealing collection of full-on-flavour savoury dishes, including roasts, grills, tarts and stews. For those who prefer a more meaty choice, opt for the ever-popular Whole Roast Rib of Beef with Roast Potatoes & Yorkshire Puddings or Pork Chops with Apple Sauce, or for a twist on a classic, try Roast Chicken Stuffed with Spiced Sour Cherries. For fish lovers, we include the perfect Spanish Paella, as well as a more contemporary Fish Stew with Cider, and then for those who prefer a vibrant vegetable-based option, the appetizing Asparagus Tart is sure to be a winner.

Baked, braised, grilled, glazed or roasted vegetables will all provide tempting sides to both traditional and more contemporary dishes, or you can go for a slightly more sophisticated side, such as Roasted Root Vegetables.

To satisfy those with a sweet tooth, it's time to perfect your dessert skills and finish the meal with a little gourmet flair. All-time prize picks include a billowing Apple Pie or Maple & Pecan Pie, but if you prefer a decadent chocolate dessert, Brownie Sundae will be a real treat. A decent dollop of whipped or clotted cream or crème fraîche, a scoop or two of luscious ice cream, or a generous drizzle of hot, creamy custard, will provide the perfect accompaniment.

# Pork Chops with Apple Sauce

*A fuss-free favourite, these succulent pork chops, served with a mildly spiced, home-made apple sauce, guarantee comfort food at its best. Serve with roasties and a selection of seasonal fresh vegetables for the perfect Sunday lunch.*

**SERVES 4**

Prepares in 20–25 minutes
Cooks in 25–30 minutes,
   plus standing

4 pork rib chops on the bone,
   each about 3 cm/1¼ inches thick,
   at room temperature
1½ tbsp sunflower oil or rapeseed oil
salt and pepper

### Apple Sauce

450 g/1 lb cooking apples, such as
   Bramley, peeled, cored and diced
4 tbsp caster sugar, plus extra, if needed
finely grated zest of ½ lemon
½ tbsp lemon juice, plus extra, if needed
4 tbsp water
¼ tsp ground cinnamon
knob of butter

1. Preheat the oven to 200°C/400°F/Gas Mark 6.

2. To make the apple sauce, put the apples, sugar, lemon zest, lemon juice and water into a heavy-based saucepan over a high heat and bring to the boil, stirring to dissolve the sugar. Reduce the heat to low, cover and simmer for 15–20 minutes, or until the apples are tender and fall apart when you mash them against the side of the pan. Stir in

the cinnamon and butter and beat the apples until they are as smooth or chunky as you like. Stir in extra sugar or lemon juice, to taste. Remove the pan from the heat, cover and keep the apple sauce warm.

3. Meanwhile, pat the chops dry and season to taste with salt and pepper. Heat the oil in a large ovenproof frying pan over a medium–high heat. Add the chops and fry for 3 minutes on each side to brown.

4. Transfer the pan to the oven and roast the chops for 7–9 minutes until cooked through and the juices run clear when you cut the chops. Remove the pan from the oven, cover with foil and leave to stand for 3 minutes. Gently reheat the apple sauce, if necessary.

5. Transfer the chops to warmed plates and spoon over the pan juices. Serve immediately, accompanied by the apple sauce.

# Roast Chicken Stuffed with Spiced Sour Cherries

*For a truly tasty twist on a classic, try these sophisticated stuffed roast chickens. Served on a large platter to impress, everyone then gets to enjoy their own whole chicken, scattered with a splendid spiced fruit-nut mixture.*

**SERVES 4**
Prepares in 35–40 minutes
Cooks in 35–45 minutes

3 garlic cloves, finely chopped
1 red chilli, deseeded
  and finely chopped
3 onions, finely sliced
2 tbsp coriander seeds
2 tsp ground cinnamon
2 tsp ground mixed spice
juice and zest of 2 lemons
4 bay leaves

100 g/3½ oz dried sour cherries
100 g/3½ oz dried cranberries
100 g/3½ oz pistachio nuts
2 tbsp extra virgin olive oil, plus
  extra for frying and drizzling
4 baby chickens or poussins
salt and pepper
roast potatoes or a salad
  of peppery leaves, to serve

1. Preheat the oven to 180°C/350°F/ Gas Mark 4. Mix the garlic and chilli with the onions. Use a pestle and mortar to crush the coriander seeds, then add to the garlic, chilli and onion mixture with the other ground spices. Add the lemon juice and zest and the bay leaves and mix everything together in a bowl with the dried fruits and nuts. Add the oil, mix well and season with salt and pepper.

2. Stuff each chicken with a generous amount of the stuffing. Heat a little oil in a heavy-based flameproof casserole. Season the chickens on the outside with salt and pepper.

3. Place the chickens in the casserole and brown both breasts and the back. Transfer the casserole to the preheated oven.

4. Roast the chickens for 30–35 minutes, or until the meat is tender, basting regularly with all the roasting juices. To check that the meat is ready, insert the point of a small knife into the thickest part of the meat – check that there is no trace of pink and the juices run clear.

5. To serve, spoon the stuffing out of the chickens and scatter over the top of the birds. Drizzle over some olive oil to add an attractive shine. Serve the chickens on a large platter surrounded by roast potatoes or with a fresh salad of bitter and peppery leaves.

# Whole Roast Rib of Beef with Roast Potatoes & Yorkshire Puddings

*For a truly stand-out traditional meat roast, rib of beef served with all the trimmings creates a popular Sunday lunch meal that is great for celebrating a special occasion with a family group or friends.*

**SERVES 8**
Prepares in 40 minutes
Cooks in 2 hours 10 minutes,
 plus resting

olive oil, for rubbing
3-kg/6 lb 8-oz joint of well-hung
  rib of beef on the bone
½ tbsp plain flour
200 ml/7 fl oz beef stock
200 ml/7 fl oz red wine
salt and pepper

### Yorkshire Puddings
250 g/9 oz plain flour, sifted
6 eggs
½ tsp salt
600 ml/1 pint milk
2 tbsp vegetable oil or lard

### Roast Potatoes
2 kg/4 lb 8 oz roasting potatoes, chopped
6 tbsp sunflower oil, goose fat or duck fat
salt and pepper

### To Serve
roasted carrots
steamed broccoli
horseradish sauce (optional)
mustard (optional)

1. For the Yorkshire puddings, mix the flour, eggs and salt together in a bowl, then gradually add the milk as you stir with a whisk. When smooth, set aside but do not chill.

2. Meanwhile, preheat the oven to 220°C/425°F/Gas Mark 7.

3. Rub a generous amount of olive oil and salt and pepper into the beef, then place in a roasting tin. Transfer to the preheated oven and roast for 30 minutes.

4. For the roast potatoes, bring a large saucepan of lightly salted water to the boil, add the potatoes, bring back to the boil and cook for 10 minutes. Drain the potatoes and toss them in oil and salt and pepper. Put them in a roasting tin in a single layer.

5. Reduce the temperature to 160°C/325°F/Gas Mark 3. Transfer the potatoes to the oven and roast with the beef for 1 hour.

6. Remove the beef from the oven and increase the oven temperature to 220°C/425°F/Gas Mark 7. Cover the beef with foil and leave to rest for at least 30 minutes.

7. Keep the potatoes in the oven. Put a 40 x 25-cm/16 x 10-inch roasting tin in the bottom of the oven to warm for the Yorkshire pudding mixture.

8. To cook the Yorkshire puddings, remove the roasting tin from the bottom of the oven and add the vegetable oil. Put it back in the oven for 5 minutes, then remove the tin and add the Yorkshire pudding batter to the base of the tin. Put it back in the hot oven for about 20 minutes.

9. Meanwhile, make the gravy. Remove the beef from the tin and stir the flour into the leftover juices, add the stock and wine, then simmer over a medium heat until reduced by about half.

10. Remove the Yorkshire pudding from the oven and divide it into eight pieces. Then remove the potatoes from the oven. Cut the rib bones off the meat and carve the beef.

11. Serve the roasted beef with the potatoes, Yorkshire puddings, gravy, carrots, broccoli and horseradish sauce and mustard, if liked.

# Grilled & Marinated Chump of Lamb

*These marvellous marinated chumps of lamb are griddled then baked to perfection and served with a moreish potato and mushroom medley to make this very tempting Sunday lunch.*

**SERVES 4**
Prepares in 45 minutes,
  plus marinating
Cooks in 35–40 minutes,
  plus resting

1 kg/2 lb 4 oz waxy potatoes,
  scrubbed or peeled
3 tbsp olive oil
250 g/9 oz mixed field
  and wild mushrooms
2 garlic cloves, finely chopped
1 tbsp chopped fresh thyme
juice of 1 lemon
1 small handful of fresh flat-leaf parsley,
  roughly chopped
salt and pepper
fresh pesto, to serve

## Lamb

4 x 200 g/7 oz chumps of lamb
4 garlic cloves, roughly crushed
2 tbsp chopped fresh rosemary
juice and zest of 1 lemon
3 tbsp olive oil

1. For the lamb, make cuts into the surfaces of the meat. Mix the garlic and rosemary with some pepper in a bowl, and rub into the cut surfaces of the meat. Place the meat in a shallow dish and add the lemon juice and zest and the olive oil. Turn over the meat a couple of times to make sure it is coated, then cover. Leave to marinate at room temperature for at least 2 hours, turning occasionally.

2. Preheat the oven to 200°C/400°F/Gas Mark 6.

3. Cut the potatoes into 5-mm/¼-inch slices. Toss with 2 tablespoons of olive oil and some salt and pepper. Place on a baking tray in a single layer and cook for about 15 minutes.

4. Meanwhile, clean the mushrooms with a small knife or brush, or a damp cloth. Do not wash. Tear into even strips. In a heavy-based saucepan, heat the remaining oil and fry the garlic and thyme until pale golden in colour. Add the mushrooms and cook over a high heat, stirring regularly.

5. Cook off all the watery liquid. If you are using a small saucepan, you might want to divide the garlic and thyme in two and fry the mushrooms in smaller batches to avoid overcrowding the pan. Fry the mushrooms for 3–4 minutes. Season with salt and pepper, add the lemon juice and cook for a further minute.

6. When the potatoes are two thirds cooked and are beginning to crisp around the edges, add the mushrooms to the baking tray and mix together. Set aside and do not place back in the oven yet.

7. Preheat the griddle pan over a high heat. Remove the meat from the marinade and pat dry. Season with salt and a little pepper.

8. Place the meat directly on the griddle pan and seal for 2 minutes on each side, then remove and place on top of the potatoes and mushrooms. Return the baking tray to the oven and roast for 15–20 minutes, until the meat is cooked through or to your liking.

9. Remove the baking tray from the oven and scatter with the chopped parsley. Allow the meat to rest for a couple of minutes before serving.

10. Slice the meat diagonally into thick slices. Serve the potatoes and mushrooms on each plate, with the lamb on top and lots of the bright green pesto splashed over the top.

# Asparagus Tart

Bake this seasonal gem in late spring or early summer and enjoy tender, fresh asparagus spears at their best. This tasty tart is great for al fresco lunchtime dining in warm weather, with a glass of chilled white wine.

**SERVES 4**
Prepares in 30–35 minutes, plus cooling
Cooks in 55 minutes–1 hour 5 minutes

375 g/13 oz ready-made shortcrust pastry, chilled
butter, for greasing
plain flour, for dusting
1 bunch thin asparagus spears
250 g/9 oz spinach leaves
3 large eggs, beaten
150 ml/5 fl oz double cream
1 garlic clove, crushed
10 small cherry tomatoes, halved
handful of chopped fresh basil
25 g/1 oz Parmesan cheese, grated
salt and pepper

1. Preheat the oven to 190°C/375°F/Gas Mark 5. Remove the pastry from the refrigerator at least 15 minutes before use, otherwise it may be brittle and difficult to handle.

2. Grease a 25-cm/10-inch tart tin with butter, then roll out the pastry on a lightly floured surface and line the tin with it. Cut off any excess pastry, prick the base with a fork, cover with a piece of baking paper and fill with baking beans. Bake blind in the preheated oven for 20–30 minutes, or until lightly browned.

3. Take the tart tin out of the oven, remove the baking paper and beans and leave to cool slightly. Reduce the oven temperature to 180°C/350°F/Gas Mark 4.

4. Meanwhile, bend the asparagus spears until they snap, and discard the woody bases.

5. Bring a large saucepan of water to the boil, add the asparagus and blanch for 1 minute, then remove and drain. Add the spinach to the boiling water, then remove immediately and drain very well.

6. Mix the eggs, cream and garlic together in a jug and season to taste with salt and pepper.

7. Lay the blanched spinach at the bottom of the pastry base, add the asparagus and the tomatoes, cut-side up, scatter over the basil, then pour the egg mixture on top.

8. Transfer to the preheated oven and bake for about 35 minutes, or until the filling has just set. Sprinkle the Parmesan cheese on top and leave to cool to room temperature before serving or serve immediately.

# Chicken, Chorizo & Seafood Paella

*Take your time to prepare the perfect paella and impress your guests with this popular full-on-flavour rice dish. It's packed with chicken, chorizo, vegetables, rice and seafood, creating a complete meal that's great for feeding a crowd.*

**SERVES 6–8**
Prepares in 35–40 minutes,
  plus soaking
Cooks in 50–55 minutes

*6 tbsp olive oil*
*6–8 boned chicken thighs*
*140 g/5 oz chorizo, diced*
*2 large onions, chopped*
*4 large garlic cloves, crushed*
*1 tsp mild or hot paprika*
*350 g/12 oz paella rice,*
  *rinsed and drained*
*100 g/3½ oz French beans, chopped*
*125 g/4½ oz frozen peas*
*1.3 litres/2¼ pints fish stock*

*½ tsp saffron threads, soaked in*
  *2 tbsp hot water*
*16 live mussels, scrubbed, debearded and*
  *soaked in salted water for 10 minutes*
*16 raw prawns, peeled and deveined*
*2 red peppers, halved and deseeded,*
  *then grilled, peeled and sliced*
*salt and pepper*
*chopped fresh parsley, to garnish*

1. Heat 3 tablespoons of the olive oil in a 30-cm/12-inch paella pan or casserole dish. Add the chicken to the casserole and cook over a medium–high heat, turning frequently, for 5 minutes, or until golden and crisp.

2. Using a slotted spoon, transfer the chicken to a bowl.

3. Add the chorizo to the casserole and cook, stirring, for 1 minute, or until beginning to crisp, then add to the chicken.

4. Heat the remaining oil in the pan, add the onions and cook, stirring, for 2 minutes. Add the garlic and paprika and cook for a further 3 minutes, or until the onions are softened but not brown.

5. Add the rice, beans and peas and stir until coated in oil. Return the chicken and chorizo and any accumulated juices to the pan. Stir in the stock, saffron and its soaking liquid, and salt and pepper to taste and bring to the boil, stirring. Reduce the heat to low and simmer, uncovered, for 15 minutes.

6. Discard any mussels with broken shells and any that refuse to close when tapped. Arrange the mussels, prawns and peppers on top. Cover and simmer for 5 minutes until the prawns turn pink and the mussels open. Discard any mussels that remain closed. Ensure the chicken is cooked through and the juices run clear by inserting a skewer into the thickest part of the meat.

7. Garnish with the parsley and serve immediately.

# Fish Stew with Cider

*For a contemporary change to a fishy favourite, try this fantastic fish stew that has an intriguing addition of cider in the creamy sorrel sauce. It's a good way to showcase sustainable fresh fish, like monkfish or cod.*

SERVES 4
Prepares in 30 minutes
Cooks in 40–45 minutes

2 tsp butter
1 large leek, thinly sliced
2 shallots, finely chopped
125 ml/4 fl oz dry cider
300 ml/10 fl oz fish stock
250 g/9 oz potatoes, diced
1 bay leaf

4 tbsp plain flour
200 ml/7 fl oz milk
200 ml/7 fl oz double cream
55 g/2 oz fresh sorrel leaves, chopped
350 g/12 oz skinless monkfish or cod
    fillet, cut into 2.5-cm/1-inch pieces
salt and pepper

1. Melt the butter in a large saucepan over a medium–low heat. Add the leek and shallots and cook for about 5 minutes, stirring frequently, until they start to soften. Add the cider and bring to the boil.

2. Stir in the stock, potatoes and bay leaf with a large pinch of salt (unless the stock is salty) and bring back to the boil. Reduce the heat, cover and cook gently for 10 minutes.

3. Put the flour in a small bowl and very slowly whisk in a few tablespoons of the milk to make a thick paste. Stir in a little more milk to make a smooth liquid.

4. Adjust the heat so the stew bubbles gently. Stir in the flour mixture and cook, stirring frequently, for 5 minutes. Add the remaining milk and half of the cream. Continue cooking for about 10 minutes, or until the potatoes are tender. Remove and discard the bay leaf.

5. Combine the sorrel with the remaining cream. Stir the sorrel cream into the stew and add the fish. Continue cooking, stirring occasionally, for about 3 minutes, or until the monkfish stiffens. Taste the stew and adjust the seasoning, if needed. Ladle into serving bowls and serve.

# Roasted Root Vegetables

SERVES 4–6

Prepares in 25 minutes, plus optional marinating

Cooks in 50–60 minutes

3 parsnips, cut into 5-cm/2-inch chunks

4 baby turnips, cut into quarters

3 carrots, cut into 5-cm/2-inch chunks

450 g/1 lb butternut squash, cut into 5-cm/2-inch chunks

450 g/1 lb sweet potatoes, cut into 5-cm/2-inch chunks

2 garlic cloves, finely chopped

2 tbsp chopped fresh rosemary

2 tbsp chopped fresh thyme

2 tsp chopped fresh sage

3 tbsp olive oil

salt and pepper

2 tbsp chopped fresh mixed herbs, such as parsley, thyme and mint, to garnish

1. Preheat the oven to 220°C/425°F/ Gas Mark 7.

2. Arrange all the vegetables in a single layer in a large roasting tin. Scatter over the garlic, rosemary, thyme and sage. Pour over the oil and season well with salt and pepper.

3. Toss all the ingredients together until they are well mixed and coated with the oil (you can leave them to marinate at this stage to allow the flavours to be absorbed).

4. Roast the vegetables at the top of the preheated oven for 50–60 minutes, or until they are cooked and nicely browned. Turn the vegetables over halfway through the cooking time.

5. Serve immediately, garnished with the mixed herbs.

# Steamed Greens with Lemon & Coriander

SERVES 4
Prepares in 15 minutes
Cooks in 6 minutes

*1 head of pointed spring cabbage,
weighing about 450 g/1 lb,
tough outer leaves discarded
200 g/7 oz baby spinach
large knob of unsalted butter
finely grated rind of ½ lemon
4 tbsp chopped fresh coriander
salt and pepper*

1. Cut the cabbage in quarters lengthways and cut out the tough stalk. Slice the quarters crossways into 2-cm/¾-inch ribbons. Steam for 3 minutes, or until starting to soften.

2. Arrange the spinach on top of the cabbage, and steam for a further 3 minutes. Drain in a colander to remove any excess liquid.

3. Tip the cabbage and spinach into a warmed serving dish. Stir in the butter, lemon rind and coriander, mixing well.

4. Sprinkle with salt and pepper and serve immediately.

# Pear & Toffee Crumble

**SERVES 4**
Prepares in 25–30 minutes
Cooks in 45–55 minutes

*1 tbsp unsalted butter, plus extra
for greasing*
*4 large pears*
*ice cream, to serve*

### Crumble Topping

*115 g/4 oz self-raising flour*
*100 g/3½ oz unsalted butter, diced*
*5 tbsp demerara sugar*
*2 tbsp finely chopped hazelnuts*

### Toffee

*3 tbsp golden syrup*
*3 tbsp demerara sugar*
*1 tbsp unsalted butter*
*2 tbsp single cream*
*½ tsp vanilla extract*

1. Preheat the oven to 200°C/400°F/ Gas Mark 6. Lightly grease an ovenproof dish.

2. To make the crumble topping, put the flour in a large mixing bowl, then use your fingertips to rub in the unsalted butter until crumbly. Stir in 4 tablespoons of the sugar and the chopped hazelnuts. Set aside.

3. To make the toffee, put the golden syrup into a small saucepan over a low heat. Add the sugar, unsalted butter, cream and vanilla extract and bring slowly to the boil. Gently simmer for 3 minutes, stirring constantly, then remove from the heat and set aside.

4. Put the unsalted butter in a frying pan and melt over a low heat. Meanwhile, peel and roughly chop the pears, then add them to the pan and cook, stirring gently, for 3 minutes. Stir in the toffee and continue to cook, stirring, over a low heat for another 3 minutes.

5. Transfer the pear-and-toffee mixture to the prepared ovenproof pie dish. Arrange the crumble evenly over the top, then sprinkle over the remaining sugar. Bake in the preheated oven for 25–30 minutes, or until the crumble is golden brown.

6. Serve immediately with ice cream.

# Apple Pie

### SERVES 6

Prepares in 45 minutes,
plus chilling

Cooks in 50 minutes

### Pastry

*350 g/12 oz plain flour, plus extra for
dusting*

*pinch of salt*

*85 g/3 oz butter, diced*

*85 g/3 oz white vegetable fat, diced*

*6 tbsp cold water*

*beaten egg or milk,
for glazing*

### Filling

*750 g–1 kg/1 lb 10 oz–
2 lb 4 oz cooking apples, peeled,
cored and sliced*

*125 g/4½ oz caster sugar, plus extra
for sprinkling*

*½ –1 tsp ground cinnamon, mixed
spice or ground ginger*

1. To make the pastry, sift the flour and salt into a bowl. Add the butter and fat and rub in with your fingertips until it resembles fine breadcrumbs. Add the water and gather together into a dough. Wrap in clingfilm and chill for 30 minutes.

2. Preheat the oven to 220°C/425°F/ Gas Mark 7. Roll out almost two thirds of the pastry thinly on a lightly floured surface and use to line a deep 23-cm/9-inch pie dish.

3. Place the apple slices, sugar and spice in a bowl and mix thoroughly. Pack the apple mixture into the pastry case; the filling can come up above the rim. Add 1–2 tablespoons of water if needed.

4. Roll out the remaining pastry on a lightly floured surface to form a lid. Dampen the edges of the pie rim with water and position the lid, pressing the edges firmly together. Trim and crimp the edges. Use the trimmings to cut out leaves or other shapes to decorate the top of the pie. Dampen and attach. Glaze the top of the pie with beaten egg, make 1–2 slits in the top and place the pie dish on a baking sheet.

5. Bake in the preheated oven for 20 minutes, then reduce to 180°C/350°F/Gas Mark 4 and bake for a further 30 minutes, or until the pastry is a light golden brown. Serve hot or cold, sprinkled with sugar.

# Maple & Pecan Pie

### SERVES 8

Prepares in 30–35 minutes,
plus chilling and cooling

Cooks in 55 minutes–
1 hour 5 minutes

### Pastry

175 g/6 oz plain flour, plus extra
for dusting

85 g/3 oz butter, diced

1 tbsp caster sugar

1 egg, beaten with 1 tbsp cold water

### Filling

85 g/3 oz butter

85 g/3 oz soft light brown sugar

150 ml/5 fl oz maple syrup

5 tbsp golden syrup

3 large eggs, beaten

1 tsp vanilla extract

200 g/7 oz pecan nuts

1. To make the pastry, sift the flour into a bowl and add the butter. Rub the butter into the flour until the mixture resembles fine breadcrumbs. Stir in the caster sugar and egg and water mixture and mix to a firm dough.

2. Turn out the dough onto a lightly floured work surface and lightly knead until smooth. Roll out and use to line a 24-cm/9½-inch loose-based tart tin. Prick the dough all over with a fork and chill in the refrigerator for 30 minutes. Meanwhile, preheat the oven to 200°C/400°F/Gas Mark 6.

3. Place the tin on a baking sheet and line with baking paper and baking beans. Bake blind in the preheated oven for 10 minutes, then remove the paper and beans and bake for a further 5 minutes, or until the pastry is light golden. Reduce the oven temperature to 180°C/350°F/Gas Mark 4.

4. To make the filling, place the butter, brown sugar, maple syrup and golden syrup in a saucepan and heat over a low heat until melted. Leave to cool for 5 minutes, then beat in the eggs and vanilla extract. Chop half of the pecan nuts and stir into the mixture.

5. Pour the mixture into the pastry case and scatter over the remaining nuts. Bake in the preheated oven for 35–45 minutes, or until the filling is just set. Serve warm or cold.

# Brownie Sundae

**SERVES 6**

Prepares in 25–30 minutes, plus cooling

Cooks in 45–55 minutes

175 g/6 oz plain chocolate

175 g/6 oz butter, plus extra for greasing

175 g/6 oz soft light brown sugar

3 eggs, beaten

115 g/4 oz self-raising flour

## Chocolate Fudge Sauce

55 g/2 oz plain chocolate, broken into pieces

55 g/2 oz soft light brown sugar

55 g/2 oz unsalted butter

3 tbsp milk

6 scoops vanilla ice cream

1 tbsp pecan nuts, chopped

6 fresh or maraschino cherries

1. Preheat the oven to 180°C/350°F/Gas Mark 4. Grease a 20-cm/8-inch square cake tin and line the tin with baking paper.

2. For the brownies, place the chocolate and butter in a large heatproof bowl set over a saucepan of simmering water and heat until melted. Cool for 5 minutes then whisk in the sugar and eggs. Sift over the flour and fold in.

3. Pour the mixture into the prepared cake tin and bake in the preheated oven for 35–40 minutes, or until risen and firm to the touch. Leave to cool in the tin for 15 minutes, then turn out onto a wire rack to cool completely.

4. For the sauce, place all the ingredients in a saucepan and heat gently, stirring all the time until melted. Bring to the boil and bubble for 1 minute. Remove from the heat and leave to cool.

5. To serve, cut the brownies into six pieces. Place each piece on a serving plate and top with a large scoop of ice cream. Spoon over the warm sauce and decorate with chopped pecan nuts and cherries.

# Weekend Brilliant Breads

Now's the time to show off your baking skills and to enjoy mastering some new bread recipes, from simple, rustic loaves to more sophisticated speciality doughs. The craft of baking bread is centuries old and it is still a hugely popular weekend pursuit today. By combining a few basic ingredients, you'll be amazed at the tempting range of breads you can create at home.

*In this chapter, we include a small but select bunch of brilliant breads and rolls which will grant you a great way to widen your baking repertoire, showcase your dexterity in baking and try your hand at creating some tempting new breads to savour and share with family and friends.*

Once you have mastered these home baking recipes, you'll be keen to improve your culinary skills further and try other techniques too.

Making bread is relaxing and enjoyable as well as being very rewarding (and tasty too!), so what better way to spend part of your weekend, than by creating and baking some delicious bread to share with family and friends? After all, who can resist the enticing, rich aromas of a freshly baked home-made loaf wafting from the kitchen, not to mention the fabulous flavour and crunch to come?

If you have plenty of time to hand, then creating these breads by hand will be most enjoyable. Kneading dough is an excellent way to relax and unwind and can be very therapeutic too as you work the ingredients together to create a smooth and elastic dough. Bread machines offer an alternative way to make bread for those with less time on their hands, but as it's the weekend and you'll hopefully have more time to spare, we concentrate our efforts on hand-made breads in this chapter.

You can make such a range of recipes – leavened or unleavened flat breads (naan, focaccia, pitta bread, chapattis, parathas, roti, tortillas, crispbreads, and so on), quick breads (soda bread, scones, muffins, teabreads) and gluten-free breads are just a few of the alternative types of bread you can make at home. So, let's get you started on this hand-picked selection of scrumptious loaves, all of which are perfect for weekend baking and sharing with others.

Popular seeded loaves include the tasty Five-seed Loaf or, for a flavour-packed loaf with a healthy twist, why not try the Granary Loaf, which is slightly sweetened with honey? There is also the classic Breakfast Bloomer Loaf, a white traditional loaf lightly dusted with flour that is delicious with butter or lightly toasted. For those who like a bit more of a challenge, the French Baguette could be the one for you – its superb flavour and texture will reward all your patience and proficiency in making it and it's great with cheese and wine.

Finally to complete our collection, for those of you who enjoy experimenting with different flours, Spelt Rolls with Spiced Fig Conserve will be the perfect challenge – this choice bake not only provides the wholesome bread rolls, it also includes a tasty conserve recipe to accompany them.

# Spelt Rolls with Spiced Fig Conserve

For those of you who like experimenting with different flours, prove your baking prowess with these special seeded spelt rolls. Make the scrumptious spiced fig conserve to accompany and your weekend breakfast is sorted!

**MAKES 16 ROLLS AND 500 G/1 LB 2 OZ CONSERVE**
Prepares in 45–50 minutes,
 plus rising, cooling and chilling
Cooks in 45 minutes

500 g/1 lb 2 oz wholemeal
 spelt flour, plus extra for dusting
1 tbsp dark muscovado sugar
1 tsp sea salt
2 tsp easy-blend dried yeast
2 tbsp sesame seeds,
 plus extra to sprinkle
2 tbsp sunflower seeds,
 plus extra to sprinkle
2 tbsp linseeds, plus extra to sprinkle
2 tbsp virgin olive oil, plus extra to grease

300–350 ml/10–12 fl oz warm water
1 tsp milk, to glaze
unsalted butter, to serve

## Spiced Fig Conserve
225 g/8 oz dried figs, diced
3 small dessert apples, cored and diced
finely grated zest and juice of 1 orange
1 tbsp light muscovado sugar
¼ tsp ground mixed spice
250 ml/9 fl oz water

1. Put the flour, dark muscovado sugar and salt in a bowl and mix well. Stir in the yeast, sesame seeds, sunflower seeds and linseeds. Add the oil, then gradually mix in enough warm water to create a soft dough, at first using a wooden spoon, then squeezing together with your hands.

2. Dust a surface with spelt flour, then knead the dough for 5 minutes. Return it to the bowl, cover with lightly oiled clingfilm and leave it to rise overnight in the refrigerator.

3. Meanwhile, to make the spiced fig conserve, put the dried figs, apples, orange zest and juice, light muscovado sugar, mixed spice and water in a saucepan. Cover and simmer over a medium heat, stirring from time to time, for 30 minutes, or until thick. Leave to cool. Sterilize a 500 g/1 lb 2 oz jar, then spoon in the conserve and leave until completely cold. Chill in the refrigerator, where it will keep for up to 10 days.

4. Line two baking sheets with baking paper. Dust a work surface with more of the spelt flour. Knead the dough briefly, then cut it into 16 pieces. Roll each piece into a ball, put one ball in the centre of each baking sheet, then arrange the others around it, leaving a little space between them.

5. Cover each sheet with lightly oiled clingfilm and leave to rise in a warm place for 40–50 minutes. Preheat the oven to 220°C/425°F/Gas Mark 7. Remove the clingfilm, brush the rolls with the milk and sprinkle with the remaining seeds. Bake in the preheated oven for 15 minutes, or until the rolls are browned and sound hollow when tapped underneath. Serve with butter and the conserve.

# Breakfast Bloomer Loaf

*This traditional crusty loaf is ideal for breakfast or as a mid-morning treat – it's great when served thickly sliced, toasted if liked, and loaded with butter and marmalade.*

**MAKES 1 LOAF**
Prepares in 20 minutes,
 plus rising and cooling
Cooks in 40–45 minutes

650 g/1 lb 7 oz strong plain flour,
  plus extra for dusting
2 tsp salt
2 tsp easy-blend dried yeast
25 g/1 oz butter, chilled and diced,
  plus extra for greasing
1 tsp caster sugar
400 ml/14 fl oz warm water
oil, for greasing

## Glaze
1 tbsp beaten egg
2 tsp milk

1. Lightly grease a large baking sheet. Mix the flour, salt and yeast in a large bowl. Add the butter and rub in to make fine breadcrumbs. Stir in the sugar.

2. Make a well in the centre of the flour mixture and pour in the warm water. Mix with a knife to make a soft, sticky dough.

3. Turn the dough onto a floured surface and knead for 10 minutes until smooth and elastic. Shape into a long oval loaf and place on the prepared baking sheet. Slash the top of the loaf six to seven times with a sharp knife. Cover loosely with lightly oiled clingfilm and leave in a warm place for 45–55 minutes until doubled in size. Preheat the oven to 230°C/450°F/Gas Mark 8.

4. To make the glaze, beat together the egg and milk with a fork. Lightly brush the glaze all over the loaf.

5. Bake the loaf in the preheated oven for 10 minutes. Reduce the oven temperature to 200°C/400°F/Gas Mark 6 and bake for a further 30–35 minutes, or until the loaf is golden and the base sounds hollow when tapped with your knuckles. Transfer to a wire rack to cool. Dust lightly with flour before serving.

3

4

5

# Granary Loaf

*This wholesome granary loaf has a lovely nutty texture and flavour. Naturally sweetened with honey, it tastes great when spread with soft cheese or when toasted and buttered.*

**MAKES 1 LOAF**
Prepares in 20 minutes,
  plus rising and cooling
Cooks in 30–35 minutes

500 g/1 lb 2 oz strong granary flour,
  plus extra for dusting
1½ tsp salt
2 tsp easy-blend dried yeast
2 tsp sunflower seeds
1 tbsp sunflower oil,
  plus extra for greasing
1 tsp runny honey
300 ml/10 fl oz warm water

1. Mix the granary flour, salt, yeast and the sunflower seeds in a large bowl and make a well in the centre.

2. Mix together the oil, honey and warm water and pour into the bowl. Mix everything together with a knife to make a soft, sticky dough.

3. Turn the dough onto a floured surface and knead for 10 minutes until smooth and elastic, adding a little more flour if the dough becomes too sticky.

4. Place in a bowl, cover with lightly oiled clingfilm and leave in a warm place for 1–1½ hours, or until doubled in size. Preheat the oven to 220°C/425°F/Gas Mark 7. Lightly grease a 900 g/2 lb loaf tin.

5. Turn the dough onto a floured surface and knead again lightly for 1 minute. Shape into an oblong and place in the loaf tin. Cover with a clean damp tea towel and leave in a warm place for about 30 minutes, or until the dough has risen above the top of the edges of the tin.

6. Dust the top of the loaf lightly with flour. Bake in the preheated oven for 30–35 minutes, or until golden and the loaf sounds hollow when tapped on the base with your knuckles. Transfer to a wire rack to cool.

# French Baguettes

*This classic French loaf is delicious with a range of cheeses and always goes well with a cup of coffee in the morning. The gluten-rich flour creates the rough, uneven holes inside the loaf.*

**MAKES 4**
Prepares in 20 minutes,
  plus rising and cooling
Cooks in 20–25 minutes

500 g/1 lb 2 oz strong white flour,
  plus extra for dusting
2 tsp sugar
2 tsp salt
15 g/½ oz fresh yeast
375 ml/13 fl oz lukewarm water

1. Mix together the flour, sugar and salt in a bowl. Make a well in the centre and crumble the yeast into it. Pour the water into the well and mix in the yeast and flour to make a smooth dough.

2. Divide the dough into four pieces and place on a baking tray. Cover with clingfilm and leave to rise for 30 minutes.

3. Transfer the dough pieces to a surface lightly dusted with flour, knock back and shape each piece into a long 5-cm/2-inch-thick roll.

4. Place the uncooked baguettes on a tea towel dusted with flour. Make folds in the towel to separate each baguette from the next. It is important that the loaves are not too close together so that they have room to rise. Cover with clingfilm and leave to rise in a warm place for about 30 minutes.

5. Preheat the oven to 240 °C/475 °F/ Gas Mark 9 and place a bowl of water in the bottom of the oven. Line a baking tray with baking paper. Place the baguettes on the prepared sheet and use a sharp knife to make five diagonal cuts in each.

6. Dust the baguettes with flour and bake in the preheated oven for 20–25 minutes, or until golden and the bases sound hollow when tapped underneath. Transfer to a wire rack to cool.

# Five-seed Loaf

*Mixed seeds add delicious flavour, texture and crunch to this ever-popular loaf. Serve it freshly baked and spread with butter for breakfast, brunch or lunch and any guests will devour this crusty bread in no time at all.*

**MAKES 1 LOAF**
Prepares in 25 minutes,
  plus rising and cooling
Cooks in 25–30 minutes

300 g/10½ oz strong wholemeal flour,
  plus extra for dusting
225 g/8 oz strong white flour
1 tsp salt
100 g/3½ oz five-seed mix
  (including sesame, pumpkin,
  sunflower, hemp and linseeds)
7 g/¼ oz easy-blend dried yeast
1 tbsp soft light brown sugar
2 tbsp sunflower oil,
  plus extra for greasing
300 ml/10 fl oz lukewarm water

1. Lightly grease a baking sheet with oil.

2. Mix the wholemeal flour, white flour, salt, seed mix and yeast in a large bowl. Stir in the sugar.

3. Mix together the oil and water to combine. Make a well in the centre of the flour mixture and pour in the liquid. Mix thoroughly with a knife to make a soft sticky dough.

4. Turn out the dough onto a lightly floured work surface and knead for 5–7 minutes, or until smooth and elastic. Shape the dough into a round ball and place on the prepared baking sheet.

5. Dust the top of the loaf with wholemeal flour and leave in a warm place for 1–1½ hours, or until doubled in size.

6. Meanwhile, preheat the oven to 220°C/425°F/Gas Mark 7. Bake the loaf in the preheated oven for 5 minutes. Reduce the oven temperature to 200°C/400°F/Gas Mark 6 and bake for a further 20–25 minutes, or until golden and the base sounds hollow when tapped with your knuckles.

7. Transfer to a wire rack to cool completely.

# Monday Morning Boosters

---

With your batteries sufficiently re-charged, you'll be feeling refreshed, revitalized and ready to face the working week ahead. Many of us are all too familiar with that sinking Monday morning feeling, but fear not as we endeavour to make Monday morning as bearable as possible. We feature a mouth-watering selection of super-charged juices, energy biscuits and power snacks, guaranteed to get you off on the right foot.

---

*It's important to try to start the week with a positive mindset as this will set the stage for the week ahead. If you can get up early and exercise first thing, this is a great way to get your circulation going and put you in the right mood for the day ahead.*

A healthy breakfast is important as it gives you vital energy and gets your day off to a good start, as well as improving performance and concentration. However, if breakfast just isn't your thing or you have limited time before you set off on your commute to work, then one of these energy boosters is a great way to keep the stomach growls at bay and nourish the body.

If you have a juicer, citrus press or blender, then it will come into its own if you need a quick energy boost to get you going in the morning. Nutritious and delicious juices and smoothies are fast and easy to make and will set you up for the day ahead, so it's well worth investing in a suitable bit of kit if this is your kind of thing.

There is a wide variety of juicers and citrus presses available, ranging in quality, efficiency and price, from simple, straightforward juicers or juice extractors to more serious, stylish, sophisticated pieces of kit. The same goes for a blender, which will also prove to be a really useful gadget to have when making other recipes such as soups, sauces and so on.

Freshly squeezed juices (and some smoothies too) are tasty and nutritious because they are loaded with fruit and vegetables, delivering a bounty of vitamins and minerals and providing an easy way to drink some of your recommended daily intake of these nutrients.

So, if you need some nifty ideas for quick and easy juices to wake you up in the morning, then look no further. We include the aptly named and delicious Dandelion Sunrise Smoothie or tantalizing Turbo Recharge Smoothie, but if you simply need some pepping up, then the refreshing Mint Rejuvenating Juice will revitalize you in no time at all.

Alternatively, when you don't have the luxury of time on your side, the Chocolate & Peanut Butter Energy Balls can be prepared ahead and will supply a much-needed energizer first thing. The Ginger & Oat No-bake Biscuits will also provide an ideal on-the-run power snack if you are short of time, or if you need the perfect pick-me-up a bit later on to keep you on the ball.

# Dandelion Sunrise Smoothie

**SERVES 1**

Prepares in 10 minutes

No cooking

*25 g/1 oz dandelion leaves*
*55 g/2 oz curly green kale*
*200 ml/7 fl oz chilled water*
*25 g/1 oz cashew nuts*
*½ tbsp coconut butter*
*1 tbsp sunflower seeds*

1. Put the dandelion leaves, kale and water into a blender and blend until smooth.

2. Add the cashew nuts, coconut butter and sunflower seeds, and blend again until the mixture is smooth and creamy.

3. Pour into a glass and serve immediately.

# Turbo Recharge Smoothie

### SERVES 1
Prepares in 15–20 minutes
No cooking

*½ honeydew melon, deseeded and roughly chopped*
*1 banana, roughly chopped*
*1 kiwi fruit, roughly chopped*
*115 g/4 oz green seedless grapes*
*small handful watercress*
*125 ml/4 fl oz unsweetened rice, almond or soya milk*
*small handful of crushed ice (optional)*

1. Put the melon, banana, kiwi fruit, grapes and watercress into a blender and blend until smooth.

2. Add the milk and crushed ice, if using, to the blender and blend again, until smooth.

3. Pour into a glass and serve immediately.

# Mint Rejuvenating Juice

### SERVES 1
Prepares in 15 minutes
No cooking

½ Galia melon, thickly sliced
85 g/3 oz baby spinach
2 sprigs fresh flat-leaf parsley
3 large stems fresh mint
small handful of ice (optional)

1. Feed the melon, spinach, parsley and two stems of mint through a juicer.

2. Half-fill a glass with ice, if using, then pour in the juice.

3. Garnish with the remaining stem of mint and serve immediately.

# Ginger & Oat No-bake Biscuits

MAKES 8

Prepares in 10–15 minutes, plus chilling

Cooks in 8–10 minutes

50 g/1¾ oz unsalted butter

200 ml/7 fl oz double cream

1 heaped tbsp unsweetened, smooth peanut butter

3 tbsp honey

1 tbsp ground ginger

200 g/7 oz large rolled oats

1. Put the butter, cream and peanut butter in a small saucepan. Bring to the boil over a medium heat, stirring occasionally from time to time. Turn the heat down to medium–low and cook for 5 minutes.

2. Tip all the remaining ingredients into the pan and stir to mix well.

3. Line a baking sheet with baking paper. Drop tablespoons of the mixture onto the tray, then cover and chill in the refrigerator for 25 minutes to harden before serving.

# Chocolate & Peanut Butter Energy Balls

*When your energy levels are low, these tempting energy balls will provide the perfect pick-me-up. They can easily be prepared ahead, so are ideal for those short of time but in need of a quick energizer first thing.*

**MAKES 8**
Prepares in 20 minutes,
 plus chilling
No cooking

*50 g/1¾ oz blanched almonds*
*60 g/2¼ oz unsweetened peanut butter*
*20 g/¾ oz unsalted peanuts,*
 *roughly chopped*
*3 tbsp linseeds*

*30 g/1 oz plain chocolate,*
 *with 85% cocoa, finely chopped*
*pinch of salt*
*1 tsp cocoa powder*

1. Put the almonds in a food processor and process for a minute, until you have the texture of rough flour.

2. Put the peanut butter, peanuts, linseeds, chocolate and a small pinch of salt into a large bowl, and mix to combine. Add the almond flour, reserving 1½ tablespoons of the mixture. Mix until you have a texture resembling chunky clay.

3. Sprinkle the remaining almond flour and the cocoa powder onto a plate and mix with a teaspoon.

4. Form a tablespoon-sized blob of the peanut mixture into a ball using your palms. Roll it in the cocoa powder mixture, then transfer to a plate. Make a further seven balls in the same way.

5. Cover with clingfilm and chill the balls in the refrigerator for at least 30 minutes before serving, or they can be stored for up to 2 days.

# Index

almonds
  Chocolate & Peanut Butter Energy Balls 219
  Cranberry & Seed Muesli 55
  Mocha Soufflés with Mascarpone 127
  Roasted Fig Tartlets with Crème de Cassis & Honey Mascarpone 122–123
Antipasti Meat Platter 151
apples
  Apple Pie 189
  Cranberry & Seed Muesli 55
  Pork Chops with Apple Sauce 171
  Spelt Rolls with Spiced Fig Conserve 197
asparagus
  Asparagus Tart 179
  Asparagus with Hollandaise Sauce 87
aubergines: Bengali Vegetable Curry 31
avocados
  Avocado, Bacon & Chilli Frittata 157
  Turkey Wraps with Avocado Salsa 75

bacon/pancetta
  Avocado, Bacon & Chilli Frittata 157
  Best Bacon Butty 65
  Chipotle Pork Fajitas 37
  Seared Scallops with Fresh Mint & Red Chilli Dressing 112–113
  Yam, Swede & Mushroom Hash 149
bananas: Turbo Recharge Smoothie 213
beansprouts
  Chicken Chow Mein 27
  Pork Pad Thai 33
beef
  Cheeseburgers with Chips 16–17
  Hearty Beef Stew with Herby Cheese Dumplings & Kale 104–105
  Rib-eye Steak, Chimichurri Sauce & Mash 99
  Whole Roast Rib of Beef with Roast Potatoes & Yorkshire Puddings 174–175
beetroots
  Beetroot Booster 56
  Beetroot Power Juice 57
  Root Vegetable Crisps with Herby Yogurt Dip 47

Black Velvet 137
blackberries
  Creamy Porridge with Blackberries 53
  Spiced Plum & Blackberry Brulées 129
Bloody Mary 165
Blueberry Booster 56
breads
  Breakfast Bloomer Loaf 199
  Five-seed Loaf 207
  French Baguettes 203
  Granary Loaf 201
  Spelt Rolls with Spiced Fig Conserve 197
broccoli: Mini Salmon & Broccoli Pies 163
burgers
  Cheeseburgers with Chips 16–17
  Lamb-cumin Pitta Burgers with Tahini Sauce 23
butternut squash
  Marinated Baked Ricotta with Roasted Vegetables 90–91
  No-crust Squash, Chorizo & Goat's Cheese Quiche 160–161
  Roasted Root Vegetables 186

cabbage: Steamed Greens with Lemon & Coriander 187
carrots
  Roasted Root Vegetables 186
  Root Vegetable Crisps with Herby Yogurt Dip 47
Champagne Cocktail 165
Champagne Sidecar 137
Champagne Sorbet 133
cheese
  Best Bacon Butty 65
  Blazing Hot Wings with Blue Cheese Dressing 41
  Cheeseburgers with Chips 16–17
  Croque Monsieur Sandwich 66
  Eggs Florentine 145
  Flatbread Pizzas with Courgette Ribbons 69
  Goat's Cheese with Honey & Walnuts 131
  Green Farro Salad with Feta 77
  Margherita Pizza 21

Marinated Baked Ricotta with Roasted Vegetables 90–91
  No-crust Squash, Chorizo & Goat's Cheese Quiche 160–161
  Pea Soup with Blue Cheese & Croûtons 67
  Savoury Vegetable Pancakes with Pesto & Braised Spinach 158–159
  Wholewheat Spinach, Pea & Feta Tart 155
  Wild Mushroom Risotto 115
  see also cream cheese
cherries
  Brownie Sundae 191
  Roast Chicken Stuffed with Spiced Sour Cherries 173
chicken
  Barbecued Asian Poussins 102–103
  Blazing Hot Wings with Blue Cheese Dressing 41
  Chicken, Chorizo & Seafood Paella 181
  Chicken Chow Mein 27
  Roast Chicken Stuffed with Spiced Sour Cherries 173
  Thai Green Chicken Curry & Udon Noodles 29
chillies
  Avocado, Bacon & Chilli Frittata 157
  Chipotle Ketchup 45
  Chipotle Mustard 45
  Chipotle Pork Fajitas 37
  Colossal Lamb Kebab with Hot Chilli Sauce 39
  Sweet Chilli Sauce 35
chocolate
  Brownie Sundae 191
  Chocolate & Peanut Butter Energy Balls 219
  Hot Chocolate Desserts & Candied Oranges 124–125
  Mocha Soufflés with Mascarpone 127
chorizo
  Chicken, Chorizo & Seafood Paella 181
  No-crust Squash, Chorizo & Goat's Cheese Quiche 160–161
coconut
  Coconut Flour Pancakes with Lemon Drizzle 59

Dandelion Sunrise Smoothie 212

Parsi-style Baked Fish Wrapped in Banana
Leaves 119

Thai Green Chicken Curry & Udon
Noodles 29

coffee

Coffee & Pecan Mini Breakfast Muffins 54

Mocha Soufflés with Mascarpone 127

courgettes

Bengali Vegetable Curry 31

Courgette Rösti with Smoked Salmon &
Eggs 147

Flatbread Pizzas with Courgette
Ribbons 69

Green Farro Salad with Feta 77

cranberries

Cranberry & Seed Muesli 55

Roast Chicken Stuffed with Spiced Sour
Cherries 173

cream cheese

Mocha Soufflés with Mascarpone 127

Roasted Fig Tartlets with Crème de
Cassis & Honey Mascarpone 122–123

Smoked Salmon Bagels 73

curry

Bengali Vegetable Curry 31

Thai Green Chicken Curry & Udon
Noodles 29


Dandelion Sunrise Smoothie 212

desserts

Apple Pie 189

Brownie Sundae 191

Champagne Sorbet 133

Hot Chocolate Desserts & Candied
Oranges 124–125

Maple & Pecan Pie 190

Mocha Soufflés with Mascarpone 127

Pear & Toffee Crumble 188

Roasted Fig Tartlets with Crème de Cassis
& Honey Mascarpone 122–123

Spiced Plum & Blackberry Brulées 129

drinks

Beetroot Power Juice 57

Black Velvet 137

Bloody Mary 165

Champagne Cocktail 165

Champagne Sidecar 137

Dandelion Sunrise Smoothie 212

Fresh Lemonade 165

Long Island Iced Tea 137

Martini 137

Mint Julep 165

Mint Rejuvenating Juice 216

Single Shot Juice Boosters 56

Turbo Recharge Smoothie 213

duck: Roast Duck Salad with Orange &
Warm Hazelnut Vinaigrette 92–93


eggs

Asparagus Tart 179

Avocado, Bacon & Chilli Frittata 157

Best Bacon Butty 65

Courgette Rösti with Smoked Salmon &
Eggs 147

Eggs Florentine 145

Huevos Rancheros 61

Lobster Salad with Herbed Mayonnaise à
la Parisienne 117

No-crust Squash, Chorizo & Goat's Cheese
Quiche 160–161

Spinach Scrambled Eggs with Wholegrain
Rye Toast 143

Yam, Swede & Mushroom Hash 149

entertaining

garnishing tips 96–97

menus 80, 82–83

preparation 84

styling food 94–95

wine tips 120–121


farro: Green Farro Salad with Feta 77

figs

Antipasti Meat Platter 151

Roasted Fig Tartlets with Crème de
Cassis & Honey Mascarpone 122–123

Spelt Rolls with Spiced Fig Conserve 197

fish & seafood

Baked Seafood with Fresh Coriander
Chutney 88–89

Beer-Battered Fish & Chips 19

Chicken, Chorizo & Seafood Paella 181

Fish Finger Sandwich with Russian
Dressing 71

Fish Stew with Cider 185

Lobster Salad with Herbed Mayonnaise à
la Parisienne 117

Parsi-style Baked Fish Wrapped in Banana
Leaves 119

see also prawns; salmon; scallops

Flatbread Pizzas with Courgette Ribbons 69

French Baguettes 203


Ginger & Oat No-bake Biscuits 217

Granary Loaf 201

grapes

Beetroot Power Juice 57

Turbo Recharge Smoothie 213

ham

Antipasti Meat Platter 151

Croque Monsieur Sandwich 66

hazelnuts

Pear & Toffee Crumble 188

Roast Duck Salad with Orange & Warm
Hazelnut Vinaigrette 92–93

Hot & Spicy Ketchup 34

Huevos Rancheros 61


kale

Dandelion Sunrise Smoothie 212

Hearty Beef Stew with Herby Cheese
Dumplings & Kale 104–105

Kale, Lemon & Chive Linguine 109

kiwi fruit

Kiwi Fruit Booster 56

Turbo Recharge Smoothie 213


lamb

Colossal Lamb Kebab with Hot Chilli
Sauce 39

Grilled & Marinated Chump of Lamb
176–177

Lamb-cumin Pitta Burgers with Tahini
Sauce 23

Slow-cooked Lamb Shanks with
  Gremolata 100–101

lemons
  Coconut Flour Pancakes with Lemon
    Drizzle 59
  Fresh Lemonade 165
  Kale, Lemon & Chive Linguine 109
  Steamed Greens with Lemon &
    Coriander 187
Lobster Salad with Herbed Mayonnaise à la
  Parisienne 117
Long Island Iced Tea 137

maple syrup
  Blazing Hot Wings with Blue Cheese
    Dressing 41
  Maple & Pecan Pie 190
Margherita Pizza 21
Martini 137
melon
  Antipasti Meat Platter 151
  Mint Rejuvenating Juice 216
  Turbo Recharge Smoothie 213
Mint Julep 165
Mint Rejuvenating Juice 216
Mocha Soufflés with Mascarpone 127
mushrooms
  Chicken Chow Mein 27
  Grilled & Marinated Chump of Lamb
    176–177
  Wild Mushroom Risotto 115
  Yam, Swede & Mushroom Hash 149
mussels
  Baked Seafood with Fresh Coriander
    Chutney 88–89
  Chicken, Chorizo & Seafood Paella 181

noodles
  Chicken Chow Mein 27
  Pork Pad Thai 33
  Thai Green Chicken Curry & Udon
    Noodles 29
nuts
  Dandelion Sunrise Smoothie 212
  Goat's Cheese with Honey & Walnuts 131

Roast Chicken Stuffed with Spiced Sour
  Cherries 173
see also almonds; hazelnuts; peanuts;
  pecan nuts

oats
  Cranberry & Seed Muesli 55
  Creamy Porridge with Blackberries 53
  Ginger & Oat No-bake Biscuits 217
oranges
  Barbecued Asian Poussins 102–103
  Greek-style Yogurt with Orange Zest &
    Toasted Seeds 52
  Hot Chocolate Desserts & Candied
    Oranges 124–125
  Roast Duck Salad with Orange & Warm
    Hazelnut Vinaigrette 92–93
  Turkey Wraps with Avocado Salsa 75

pancakes
  Coconut Flour Pancakes with Lemon
    Drizzle 59
  Savoury Vegetable Pancakes with Pesto &
    Braised Spinach 158–159
parsnips
  Roasted Root Vegetables 186
  Root Vegetable Crisps with Herby Yogurt
    Dip 47
pasta: Kale, Lemon & Chive Linguine 109
pastry
  Apple Pie 189
  Asparagus Tart 179
  Maple & Pecan Pie 190
  Mini Salmon & Broccoli Pies 163
  No-crust Squash, Chorizo & Goat's Cheese
    Quiche 160–161
  Roasted Fig Tartlets with Crème de
    Cassis & Honey Mascarpone 122–123
  Wholewheat Spinach, Pea & Feta Tart 155
peanuts
  Chocolate & Peanut Butter Energy
    Balls 219
  Ginger & Oat No-bake Biscuits 217
  Pork Pad Thai 33
  Pear & Toffee Crumble 188

peas
  Bengali Vegetable Curry 31
  Chicken, Chorizo & Seafood Paella 181
  Green Farro Salad with Feta 77
  Mushy Peas 19
  Pea Soup with Blue Cheese & Croûtons 67
  Wholewheat Spinach, Pea & Feta
    Tart 155
pecan nuts
  Brownie Sundae 191
  Coffee & Pecan Mini Breakfast Muffins 54
  Maple & Pecan Pie 190
peppers
  Barbecued Asian Poussins 102–103
  Chicken, Chorizo & Seafood Paella 181
  Chicken Chow Mein 27
  Chipotle Pork Fajitas 37
  Huevos Rancheros 61
pizza
  Flatbread Pizzas with Courgette
    Ribbons 69
  Margherita Pizza 21
plums
  Beetroot Power Juice 57
  Spiced Plum & Blackberry Brulées 129
Popcorn, Rosemary, Sea Salt &
  Sesame 46
pork
  Barbecued Pulled Pork with Sweet Potato
    Mash 107
  Chipotle Pork Fajitas 37
  Pork Chops with Apple Sauce 171
  Pork Pad Thai 33
potatoes
  Beer-Battered Fish & Chips 19
  Bengali Vegetable Curry 31
  Cheeseburgers with Chips 16–17
  Fish Stew with Cider 185
  Grilled & Marinated Chump of Lamb
    176–177
prawns
  Baked Seafood with Fresh Coriander
    Chutney 88–89
  Chicken, Chorizo & Seafood Paella 181
  Pork Pad Thai 33

Rib-eye Steak, Chimichurri Sauce & Mash 99

rice

Chicken, Chorizo & Seafood Paella 181

Wild Mushroom Risotto 115

Roasted Root Vegetables 186

Root Vegetable Crisps with Herby Yogurt
Dip 47

salads

Green Farro Salad with Feta 77

Lobster Salad with Herbed Mayonnaise à
la Parisienne 117

Marinated Baked Ricotta with Roasted
Vegetables 90–91

Roast Duck Salad with Orange & Warm
Hazelnut Vinaigrette 92–93

salmon

Courgette Rösti with Smoked Salmon &
Eggs 147

Mini Salmon & Broccoli Pies 163

Smoked Salmon Bagels 73

sausage

Antipasti Meat Platter 151

see also chorizo

scallops

Baked Seafood with Fresh Coriander
Chutney 88–89

Seared Scallops with Fresh Mint & Red
Chilli Dressing 112–113

seeds

Bengali Vegetable Curry 31

Chocolate & Peanut Butter Energy
Balls 219

Cranberry & Seed Muesli 55

Dandelion Sunrise Smoothie 212

Five-seed Loaf 207

Greek-style Yogurt with Orange Zest &
Toasted Seeds 52

Spelt Rolls with Spiced Fig Conserve 197

soup: Pea Soup with Blue Cheese &
Croûtons 67

soured cream

Coffee & Pecan Mini Breakfast Muffins 54

Turkey Wraps with Avocado Salsa 75

Spelt Rolls with Spiced Fig Conserve 197

spinach

Asparagus Tart 179

Eggs Florentine 145

Green Farro Salad with Feta 77

Mint Rejuvenating Juice 216

Savoury Vegetable Pancakes with Pesto
& Braised Spinach 158–159

Spinach Scrambled Eggs with Wholegrain
Rye Toast 143

Steamed Greens with Lemon &
Coriander 187

Wholewheat Spinach, Pea & Feta Tart 155

storecupboard ingredients 42–43

swedes: Yam, Swede & Mushroom
Hash 149

Sweet Chilli Sauce 35

sweet potatoes

Barbecued Pulled Pork with Sweet Potato
Mash 107

Marinated Baked Ricotta with Roasted
Vegetables 90–91

Rib-eye Steak, Chimichurri Sauce &
Mash 99

Roasted Root Vegetables 186

Root Vegetable Crisps with Herby Yogurt
Dip 47

Thai Green Chicken Curry & Udon
Noodles 29

tomatoes

Antipasti Meat Platter 151

Asparagus Tart 179

Flatbread Pizzas with Courgette
Ribbons 69

Hot & Spicy Ketchup 34

Huevos Rancheros 61

Margherita Pizza 21

Slow-cooked Lamb Shanks with
Gremolata 100–101

Turkey Wraps with Avocado Salsa 75

Wholewheat Spinach, Pea & Feta Tart 155

tortillas

Chipotle Pork Fajitas 37

Turkey Wraps with Avocado Salsa 75

Turbo Recharge Smoothie 213

Turkey Wraps with Avocado Salsa 75

turnips: Roasted Root Vegetables 186

watercress

Barbecued Asian Poussins 102–103

Roast Duck Salad with Orange & Warm
Hazelnut Vinaigrette 92–93

Turbo Recharge Smoothie 213

wine tips 120–121

Yam, Swede & Mushroom Hash 149

yogurt

Greek-style Yogurt with Orange Zest &
Toasted Seeds 52

Root Vegetable Crisps with Herby Yogurt
Dip 47

Spiced Plum & Blackberry Brulées 129

Yorkshire Puddings 174–175